Heavy-lift Aircraft in History

On 27 April 2005, an aircraft lifted away from the runway of Toulouse-Blagnac Airport under the power of four massive Rolls-Royce Trent 900 turbofan engines. It carried a six-man crew, it was making its first flight, and it was making history. For this was the Airbus A380, the largest passenger aircraft in the world.

A briefing on success and failure

The A380 is at the apex of a long line of very large aircraft designs extending all the way back to the 1920s. The beginning of commercial aviation initiated a desire to develop both military and civil aircraft capable of transporting large and heavy payloads over long distances. The concept had both advantages and drawbacks. Producing a type of very large aircraft, although it can result in better fuel efficiency and provide a greater space to accommodate both payload and passengers, can create problems not present in smaller designs, such as structural integrity, flight control response and sufficient power to cope with all aspects of the flight regime.

Early aero-engines failed to provide the necessary power to lift very large heavier-than-air machines. The Beardmore Inflexible of the 1920s, a massive three-engine aircraft with a wing span of 157ft 6in (48.05m) and using a stressed-skin construction technique developed by the German Rohrbach company, was a good example. The sole example was built in sections by William Beardmore and Company at Dalmuir, Scotland, between 1925 and 1927. It was shipped by sea to Felixstowe and then delivered by road to the Aeroplane and Armament Experimental Establishment at Martlesham Heath, where it first flew on 5 March 1928. The aircraft was structurally advanced for its time and had good flying qualities, but its three 620hp Rolls-Royce Condor engines did not develop sufficient power to cope with an all-up weight of 37,000lb (17,000kg) and it was abandoned.

The massive Beardmore Inflexible was a concept far ahead of its time, but one that suffered from underdeveloped engines that doomed it from the outset. (RAF Historical Society)

Top: The Dornier Do X in flight over San Diego. It was the largest, heaviest and most powerful flying boat in the world when it was built, but only three were produced. (Bundesarchiv)

Above: Passengers boarding Russia's giant Maksim Gorki airliner. It first flew in June 1934 and was destroyed in a mid-air collision the following year. (TASS)

The relative success of Germany's Zeppelin airships during the First World War persuaded the postwar German government that commercial airships were the solution to long-range air travel, but that dream died in the wreckage of the airship *Hindenburg*, which exploded at Lakehurst, New Jersey, in 1937. To this day, the *Hindenburg* and her sister ship, *Graf Zeppelin*, remain the largest lighter-than-air craft ever built. In the heavier-than-air field, Germany's Dornier Do X flying boat of 1929, weighing in at just over 108,000lb (49,000kg) and powered by 12 radial engines, was the largest, heaviest and most powerful flying boat in the world when it was built, but only three were produced.

The Do X was surpassed in size during the interwar years by Russia's Tupolev ANT-20 Maksim Gorki, which weighed 75 tonnes and had a wing span of 156ft 10in (47.8m). This six-engine giant first flew in June 1934 and could carry 72 passengers, but its career was short-lived. It was lost in May 1935 when it collided with an I-5 fighter.

One of the largest aircraft of its time, and a true commercial success story, was the Boeing Model 314 flying boat. It entered service with Pan American Airways in 1938 and was capable of crossing the Atlantic nonstop with 74 passengers. It had a loaded weight of 84,000lb (38,000kg) and its massive 152ft (46.36m) wing was based on that of a cancelled heavy bomber, the Boeing XB-15. On 17 June 1939 the first Model 314, *Yankee Clipper*, made the first scheduled passenger-carrying run over the North Atlantic from New York to Southampton via Newfoundland. On the 28th a sister aircraft, *Dixie Clipper*, flew over the southern route to Marseille. The first aircraft carried 18 passengers, the second twenty-two. Twelve Model 314s were built, undertaking regular weekly services over the Atlantic, and went on to have distinguished wartime careers.

Subsequently, the size and weight of aircraft were dictated by the wartime demands of the military. The largest and heaviest aircraft in the world in the mid-war

The Boeing 314 Clipper was one of the largest aircraft of its time and revolutionized transatlantic air travel. Twelve aircraft were built and were commercially successful, also serving as military transports during the Second World War. (Boeing)

years was the Boeing B-29 Superfortress, with a wing span of 141ft 2.75in (43.05m) and a maximum takeoff weight of 124,000lb (56,246kg), but this was surpassed by Germany's Junkers Ju 390 six-engine bomber/transport, which first flew in October 1943 and had a wing span of 165ft 1in (50.32m) and a maximum takeoff weight of 166,450lb (75,500kg). Only one prototype was completed. It was a Blohm & Voss flying boat, though that smashed the wartime record for size and weight. This was the Bv 238, the heaviest aircraft ever built when it first flew in 1944 and the largest aircraft produced by any of the Axis powers. Its massive wing had a span of 197ft 5in (60.17m) and its maximum takeoff weight was 220,462lb (100,000kg). The sole prototype was destroyed just before the end of the war and a projected transport version, the Bv 250, was never completed.

Yet even the Bv 238 was eclipsed by another design, the massive Hughes H-4 Hercules, designed and built by the Hughes Aircraft Company as a prototype strategic airlift flying boat. In 1942 the US War Department requirement was for an aircraft that could cross the Atlantic with a very large payload and avoid the huge losses of shipping then being suffered at the hands of Germany's U-boats. Construction of the H-4, nicknamed the 'Spruce Goose' because it was built from wood, proceeded slowly, and the only prototype was not completed until well after the war was over. With a huge wingspan of 320ft 11in (97.54m) and with a designed loaded weight of 400,000lb (180,000kg), it made only one short flight on 2 November 1947 at Long Beach, California. It remained airborne for 26 seconds at 70 feet (21m) and covered about a mile over the water, achieving a speed of 135mph (217km/h). Howard Hughes, called before a Senate Committee to justify the massive development cost of the H-4, stated:

'The Hercules was a monumental undertaking. It is the largest aircraft ever built. It is over five stories tall with a wingspan longer than a football field. That's more than a city block. Now, I put the sweat of my life into this thing. I have my reputation all rolled up in it and I have stated several times that if it's a failure, I'll probably leave this country and never come back. And I mean it.'

And so it was to be. The Hughes H-4, in one aircraft project, encapsulated all the difficulties attending the design of super-sized aircraft in that era. One of the main difficulties was power; despite the fact that it was powered by eight 3,000hp Pratt & Whitney radial engines, and although its airworthiness was proven by its one short flight, the H-4's lifting capacity and other

The mighty Bv 238 flying boat was the heaviest aircraft ever built when it first flew in 1944. (Bundesarchiv)

The Boeing B-29 Superfortress long-range strategic bomber was the largest and heaviest aircraft in the mid-war years, its operations culminating in the dropping of atomic bombs on Hiroshima and Nagasaki. (Boeing)

The Junkers Ju 390 prototype in flight. It first flew in October 1938 and was said to have flown to within 12 miles of New York on an evaluation flight, but this was never substantiated. (Bundesarchiv)

The mighty Hughes Hercules encapsulated, in a single airframe, most of the problems attending the design of super-sized aircraft. The main problem was lack of power. (NASM)

The Saunders-Roe Princess brought an end to the development of commercial flying boats in the United Kingdom. Only one of the three aircraft built flew, in August 1942. (San Diego Air & Space Museum)

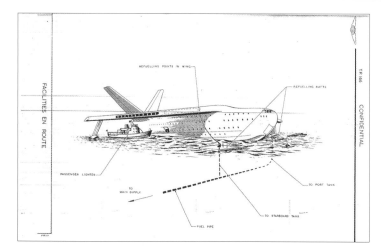

A confidential company sketch illustrating the main features of the SARO P.192 Queen project.

performance estimates were never tested. It never flew again, and ended its days as a museum piece.

The end of the very large commercial flying boat came in the 1950s with the cancellation of Britain's Saunders-Roe Princess flying boat programme. Three of these massive boats were built following a specification issued in 1946, but only the first ever flew, on 22 August 1952. The Princess could accommodate 100 passengers on transcontinental flights. The construction programme ran into difficulties, and in 1951 BOAC announced that it no longer intended to adopt the new

flying boat. It had been intended to replace the small and successful Short C Class boats, having opted to use only land planes in its fleet. The Princess was powered by ten Bristol Proteus turboprop engines, four of which were in coupled pairs; its wing span was 219ft 6in (66.90m) and maximum takeoff weight was 345,025lb (1556,501kg).

Even as the events that signalled the demise of the Princess were unfolding, however, the talented and innovative Saunders-Roe design team were still considering a jet-powered passenger flying boat project that would have put all other commercial designs in the shade. This was the mighty SARO P.192 Queen. The concept had its origin in an interest expressed by representatives of the P&O shipping line for an aircraft that could carry 1,000 passengers under the conditions and comfort of a transatlantic ocean liner. SARO's proposal involved a 670-ton flying boat powered by 24 Rolls-Royce Conway turbojets, each developing a thrust of 18,500lb (8,400kg). The aircraft was designed to have a cruising speed of 450mph (720km/h) at an altitude between 30,000 and 39,000 feet (9,000 and 12,000m). Planned range was 2,000 miles (3,400km), sufficient to carry the P.192 from London to Sydney via Cairo, Karachi, Calcutta, Singapore and Darwin.

Although the technology that went into the design of the Bristol Brabazon was very advanced, the concept dated from the Second World War and the aircraft was two years behind schedule before it flew in 1949. (Bob Sharp)

The fuselage would have been divided into five decks, with the passengers accommodated in six-place compartments featuring seats that could be converted into sleeping berths. First class passengers would have had their own bars, dining rooms and washrooms. A well-equipped galley would serve all the decks by means of lifts. The crew was to comprise seven flight personnel with their own rest quarters and 40 cabin crew, as well as a purser, as on a liner. The engines were to be installed on a high-mounted wing to avoid ingesting spray and would have two sets of intakes, one mounted above the wing when the aircraft was on the water, and another in the leading edge for sustained flight. Ship-type rudders were to be fitted to assist manoeuvring on the water.

However, neither P&O nor the British taxpayer was willing to finance such a project. It never left the drawing board.

In 1953 the axe also fell on another very large British airliner project, the Bristol Brabazon. Britain's only venture into the field of super-large passenger/transport aircraft in the immediate postwar years crystallized in the Bristol Brabazon, an aircraft technologically far ahead of its time that had its origins of 1943, following the recommendations of a committee chaired by Lord Brabazon of Tara, for whom the aircraft took its name. The role of the committee was to recommend the types of aircraft that would be best suited for production by the British civil aviation industry after the war, and the Brabazon project, designed to carry 100 passengers nonstop from London to New York at 300mph, was particularly attractive. However, practical, economic and, above all, political factors conspired to prevent the aircraft going into production. The Brabazon Mk 1 prototype flew for the first time on 4 September 1949, two years behind schedule and powered by eight Bristol Centaurus radial engines. Designs for a Mk 2 version were drawn up, which would be powered by four 7,000ehp Coupled-Proteus turboprops, but this was shelved in 1952. The government decided to abandon the project in 1953, partly due

to wildly escalating development costs and problems with the Proteus engine. The Mk 1 Brabazon had a wingspan of 230ft (70m) and a planned maximum takeoff weight of 290,000lb (130,000kg).

In the military field, the immediate postwar years produced the Convair B-36. Development had begun in 1941 in response to a requirement for a strategic bomber capable of reaching targets in Europe nonstop from bases in the United States. The first bomber with a truly global strategic capability to serve with any air force, the B-36, flew for the first time on 8 August 1946. An initial production batch of 22 B-36As was built, the first being delivered to Strategic Air Command in the summer of 1947. The second production model, the B-36B, was powered by six Pratt & Whitney R-4630-41 engines with water injection, and was fully combat-equipped. The most important production version was the B-36D, which had four J47 turbojets as well as its six radial engines. Twenty-two aircraft were built and 64 earlier models brought up to B-36D standard. It was followed by the B-36F (28 built), B-36H (81 built) and B-36J (33 built). Reconnaissance variants were the RB-36D, RB-36E and RB-36H. With a wingspan of 230ft (70.12m) and a maximum takeoff weight of 410,000lb (186,000kg), it formed the core of the USAF's strategic bomber fleet until the deployment of an all-jet bomber force.

Although of poor quality, this image is of interest as it shows the giant aircraft with a damaged wingtip, the result of a ground handling accident. (Bob Sharp)

The first bomber with a truly global strategic capability, the Convair B-36 first flew in August 1946. The most important production version was the B-36D, which had four J47 turbojets as well as its six radial engines. (NASM)

Developed from the B-36, the Convair XC-99 was the largest piston-engine transport aircraft ever built. The sole prototype was used as a heavy-lift transport by the USAF from 1950 to 1957. (NASM)

Inevitably, and relevant to the theme of this narrative, the huge B-36 produced a transport spin-off in the Convair XC-99, a prototype heavy-cargo aircraft that shared the same wings and some other structural features with the bomber. The largest piston-engine transport aircraft ever built, the XC-99 had a design capacity of 1,00,000lb (45,000kg) of cargo or accommodation for 400 fully equipped troops in two cargo decks. A cargo lift was installed to facilitate loading. The aircraft

flew for the first time on 24 November 1947 and was delivered to the US Air Force in May 1949. It flew numerous transport missions with the USAF between 1950 and 1957, when it was retired. It was eventually allocated to the National Museum of the United States Air Force.

In the USAF, the ultimate in heavy piston-engine transport aircraft was the Douglas C-124A Globemaster II. First flown in November 1949, it served as the USAF's primary heavy-lift transport during the 1950s and early 1960s, until replaced by the jet-powered Lockheed C-141 Starlifter. Powered by four 3,800hp Pratt & Whitney radial engines, the C-124A had a wingspan of 174ft 1.5in (53.073m) and a maximum takeoff weight of 194,500lb (88,224kg).

After the C-124A and the C-141, the USAF's Military Airlift Command took delivery of what was then the largest jet-powered transport aircraft in service anywhere in the world. This was the Lockheed C-5A Galaxy, first flown in June 1968. Its wingspan was 222ft 9in (67.89m) and its maximum takeoff weight was a staggering 920,000lb (418,000kg). It was powered by four General Electric turbofan engines, each developing 51,000lb of thrust.

Meanwhile, Soviet designers had been concentrating on the development of

The USAF's principal heavy-lift transport in the 1950s and early 1960s was the Douglas C-124A Globemaster II, which first flew in November 1949. (USAF)

The C-124A was replaced in USAF service by the turbojet-powered Lockheed C-141 Starlifter; it brought a new dimension to the USAF's rapid reinforcement commitment. (USAF)

First flown in June 1968, the Lockheed C-5A Galaxy was at that time the largest jet-powered transport aircraft in the world. (Lockhed Martin)

turboprop-powered aircraft to meet the USSR's civil and military long-range heavy-airlift requirements. A few days before the 40th anniversary of the Russian Revolution, the largest Soviet turboprop aircraft of the time and the largest commercial aircraft in the world made its first flight. It was the Tupolev Tu-114 Rossiya; Andrei Tupolev's response to a requirement for an aircraft cabable of literally spanning the globe. Based on the Tu-95 Bear strategic bomber, using the same wing mounted low on the fuselage so that the passenger cabin was unobstructed by the wing main spar structure. It broke new ground in the history of air transportation. One of its most successful routes was the joint Aeroflot–Japan Air Lines service between Moscow and Tokyo which was operated with mixed Russian/Japanese crews. The performance of the airliner, given the NATO reporting name Cleat, was not outstanding. However, its load-carrying and speed made it the USSR's prestige airliner throughout the 1960s.

At the Paris Air Show in June 1965, designer Oleg K. Antonov revealed his latest creation: it stunned the aviation world. The huge An-22 heavy transport, first flown in February that year, was soon to enter service with both Aeroflot and the Soviet Air Forces, which used it to transport

large cargoes such as missiles on tracked launchers and dismantled aircraft. When it made its debut, the An-22 was the heaviest aircraft ever built. Fifty examples were completed up to 1974 when production ended.

But Antonov had more surprises in store a few years later, the first being the Antonov An-124 Ruslan. One of the largest aircraft ever built. The mighty An-124 transport, designed for very heavy-lift, proved a winning design from the outset. Dubbed Condor under the NATO reporting system, it was more popularly and correctly known by its Russian name, Ruslan, which first appeared on the second prototype.

The turboprop-powered Tupolev Tu-114 was built in response to an Aeroflot requirement for an airliner with global capability. It was based on the Tu-95 strategic bomber. (Air-Britain/ Dave Welch)

Built as both a civil and military transport, the Antonov An-22 was the heaviest transport aircraft ever built when it first appeared in the mid-1960s. The prototype, as seen here on its maiden flight, is still in its natural metal finish. (Antonov State Enterprise)

One of the largest aircraft ever built, the Antonov An-124 Ruslan was a great success, providing an unparalleled heavy-lift capability for Aeroflot and other operators. (Antonov State Enterprise)

The massive An-225 Mriya seen at the Paris Air Show, le Bourget, with Russia's planned Buran (Snowstorm) space shuttle mounted on its back. (Antonov State Enterprise)

A wind-tunnel model of Russia's proposed new heavy-lift transport, the Elephant, minus its tail unit. Essentially, it resembles a scaled-up An-124. (TsAGI)

(Ruslan is the giant folk-hero of Russian literature and music). The first prototype An-124 began its flight test programme on 26 December 1982; the aircraft was making proving flights on Aeroflot's routes by the end of 1985. By 1991 at least 23 An-124s were in service and the Antonov bureau had formed a special company to sell cargo space all over the world.

Although the concept of a transport aircraft to carry orbital space vehicles between locations on the ground was pioneered by NASA's Boeing 747/Space Shuttle combination, the idea reached a new peak of development in the former Soviet Union. Following trials with a much-modified Myasishchev Mya-4 Bison bomber (named VM-t Atlant), which proved that the piggyback method of transporting heavy and outsized loads was feasible by carrying components of the Energiya booster that would be used to launch the Russian space shuttle, Buran (Snowstorm), the massive Antonov An-225 Mriya (Dream) made its appearance in 1988. The An-225 was developed specifically with the Russian space programme in mind and was the first aircraft in the world to be flown at a gross weight of 1,000,000lb (453,000kg).

During 2020, indications were that the story of Antonov's heavy-lifters was starting a new chapter. Russia's Central Aerohydrodynamic Institute – TsAGI – revealed that a potential replacement for the An-124 was under development and that a model was at the wind tunnel testing stage. Known unofficially as the Elephant, the proposed aircraft is designed to carry heavy loads over a range of up to 4,450 miles (7,000km) at an airspeed of 528mph (850km/h). Maximum payload would be 180 tonnes, compared with the An-124's 120 tonnes. The aircraft would need a 9,843-foot (3,000m) runway. It would be powered by four PD-35 turbofan engines, each capable of developing 33 to 40 tonnes of thrust.

Enter the widebodies

The age of the widebodied jet transport came into being on 9 February 1969, with the first flight of the Boeing 747 Jumbo Jet, developed initially to rival and surpass the 'stretched' version of the Douglas DC-8. Numerous variants of the 747 were subsequently produced. The first production model, the 747-100, went into service with Pan American on the London–New York route on 22 January 1970. Originally planned as a double-decker, the 747 eventually became essentially a single-deck design, seating 385 people in the basic passenger model, including 16 in an upper-deck lounge.

In October 1970 Boeing flew the first Model 747-200, with a greater fuel capacity and increased gross weight. The basic passenger version was the Model 747-200B, while the Model 747-200F was a dedicated cargo version with no windows and a hinged nose for straight-in loading of pallets and containers. Variants produced include the 747SP, a special-performance, long-range version with a shortened fuselage and an enlarged tail fin. Among other notable flights, a Pan American 747SP flew around the world in one day, 22 hours and 50 minutes at an average speed of 503mph (809km/h) and another traversed the globe by crossing both poles.

The second widebodied, high-density aircraft to enter airline service was the McDonnell Douglas DC-10, which flew for the first time on 29 August 1970, and production aircraft entered service on 5 August the following year with American Airlines on the Los Angeles-Chicago route. An extended-range variant, the DC-10-30, flew on 21 June 1972; intended for intercontinental routes, this had more powerful engines, a third main undercarriage unit and increased-span wing; it was followed by several other variants, including the more powerful Series 40. Later, the aircraft was redesignated MD-11; later versions had a stretched fuselage to provide greater accommodation

The Boeing 747 Jumbo Jet was originally planned as a double-deck design. The first production model, seen here, was the 747-100, which entered service with Pan American on the London–New York route on 22 January 1970. (Pan Am)

The second widebodied, high-density aircraft to enter airline service was the McDonnell Douglas DC-10, which flew for the first time on 29 August 1970. Production aircraft entered service on 5 August the following year with American Airlines on the Los Angeles–Chicago route. (NASM)

In the 1990s McDonnell Douglas proposed an airliner, the MD-12, which would be similar in size to the Boeing 747 but with greater passenger capacity. It was first conceived as a trijet, similar to the MD-11, but later stretched to a four-jet design. However, no interest was forthcoming and the project was cancelled. (McDonnell Douglas)

The market requirements that had led to the development of the McDonnell Douglas DC-10 also resulted in the Lockheed TriStar high-density jet airliner programme. Pictured here is a converted TriStar, named *Stargazer*, used by Orbital Sciences to launch Pegasus rockets into Earth's orbit. (Orbital Sciences)

Above and below: The Ilyushin Il-86 was Russia's first widebody airliner design. It first flew on 28 September 1988 and made its international debut at the Paris Air Show the following June. The Il-86 was by no means as successful as its western counterparts. (Novosti)

This Ilyushin Il-96 is used as the personal transport of the Russian president and his entourage, as indicated by the name *Rossiya* (Russia) on its fuselage. (Jet Photos)

for both passengers and luggage, while the wings were lengthened and incorporated winglets. The MD-11's overall design was more advanced than the DC-10's, resulting in greater efficiency, while the earlier analogue cockpit display was replayed by multi-function CRT displays.

In the 1990s McDonnell Douglas proposed an airliner, the MD-12, which would be similar in size to the Boeing 747 but with greater passenger capacity. It was first conceived as a trijet, similar to the MD-11, but later stretched to a four-jet design. However, no interest was forthcoming and the project was cancelled.

The market requirements that had led to the development of the McDonnell Douglas DC-10 also resulted in the Lockheed TriStar high-density jet airliner programme. The project, designated L-1101, was launched in March 1968, by which time 144 orders and options were in place. The first aircraft flew on 16 November 1970. The initial version was the Lockheed L-1011-1 which entered regular airline service with Eastern Air Lines on 26 April 1972. By late 1973 some 56 were in service, with orders and options for a further 199. It was not enough, because by this time the DC-10 was making inroads into the intercontinental market, so Lockheed set about increasing the TriStar's range and payload, starting with the L-1011-100 series. Powered by three Rolls-Royce RB.211 turbofans, this became the most adaptable of the TriStar series, but it failed to match the range and payload capability of the DC-10 Series 30. In an attempt to bring about a radical improvement of the TriStar's range capability, Lockheed introduced the L-1011-500, this aircraft received Federal Aviation Administration (FAA) certification in December 1979.

The Soviet Union emerged on to the widebody stage in December 1976 with the first flight of the Ilyushin Il-86. Aeroflot began services with the type in October 1977, but these were mostly restricted to destinations within the USSR because of the airliner's poor range. This resulted in the development of an improved version, the Il-96, which was virtually a new design. Almost the only components left unaltered, or only slightly modified, were major sections of the fuselage (though this was made much shorter) and the four units of the landing gear. The first prototype of the Il-96 flew on 28 September 1988, and the type made its international debut at the Paris Air Show the following June. Aeroflot placed orders for about 100 aircraft for service on its long-range, high-density routes both at home and overseas, but only 16 were in service in September 2006. Further developments of the type are the Il-96M with 350 seats for medium-range sectors, and the Il-90 twin-engine version.

Airbus Rising

In the early 1970s Boeing's apparent monopoly of the civil airliner market began to come under serious and sustained attack by the European consortium, Airbus Industrie, which within a decade would capture over 55 percent of the world market for twin-aisle transport aircraft.

Airbus Industrie was a latecomer to the commercial airliner market and initially struggled to win orders away from the well-established US giants, Boeing and McDonnell Douglas. Part of Airbus's strategy for success was to offer customers distinct families of aircraft that could be tailored to meet a wide range of performance and capacity demands. In 1972 the company flew the Airbus A300, the first widebody twin-engine commercial aircraft to enter service. Initial sales were poor, but then Airbus launched the A300B4, designed for medium-haul routes. Four aircraft were taken by Eastern Air Lines on a six-month lease, beginning in late 1977. The airline was so impressed by the aircraft that it bought the original four, together with 25 more. It was the beginning of the Airbus success story; by 1978, Airbus had secured orders from other American airlines and had come second only to Boeing in widebody sales. Within three years it had pushed Boeing into second place.

The A310 was a shorter version of the A300 with modified wings, and tended to be overshadowed by the A320, the model that heralded the age of the truly high-technology airliner and the model that guaranteed Airbus's position as a leading participant in the world airliner market. The A320 had secured 400 orders before it even flew. The A318, A319 and A321 were short-haul derivatives, while the twin-jet A330 and four-jet A340 were long-range

The Airbus A300, seen here in the livery of Federal Express (FedEx) was the first twin-engine commercial widebody to enter service. (Airbus)

The Airbus A320 was the model that guaranteed the company's place as a leading participant in the world airliner market and ushered in the age of the true high-technology airliner. This example is operated by Atlantic Airways, the national airline of the Faroe Islands. (C. Brinkmann)

First flown in October 1991 the Airbus A340 is a four-jet long-range member of the Airbus family. Three hundred and eighty were built before production ended in November 2011. (Airbus)

models. Before 2005, the latter were the largest and arguably the most important members of the Airbus family; then along came the A380.

A380: design concepts

The first flight was the culmination of design studies that had started in 1988, the specific task being to challenge the domination of America's Boeing 747 in the long-haul market. Airbus assembled four teams of designers, one from each of its partners – Aérospatiale, British Aerospace, Deutsche Aerospace AG and

Construcciones Aeronáuticas SA (CASA) – each of which was asked to draw up design proposals for what was then known as the UHCA (Ultra-High-Capacity Airliner). Work proceeded in strict secrecy as other companies were known to be pursuing similar studies. McDonnell Douglas, for example, was examining the MD-12 design concept, in essence a much larger version of its successful MD-11 (formerly Douglas DC-10) Trijet, while Lockheed was exploring the possibility of a Very Large Commercial Transport (VLCT) as a follow-on to its L1101 TriStar.

The project was announced at the 1990 Farnborough Air Show, the stated goal being that the new aircraft's operating costs would be 15 percent lower than those of the Boeing 747-400. The designs were submitted in 1992 and the most competitive submissions were selected to form the basis for the new airliner. However, various options were considered to exploit what was after all deemed to be a very limited market. One of these, tabled in January 1993, involved a feasibility study with Boeing, the plan being to investigate the possibility of a partnership to develop a VLCT.

Despite the fact that only two airlines had expressed public interest in purchasing such

Above: One of the A3XX design studies featured an aircraft with a twin-tail configuration as seen in this computer image. (Airbus)

Right: A mock-up of the Airbus A380, one of several produced during the aircraft's development path. (Airbus)

an aircraft, Airbus had announced a year earlier, in June 1994, its intention to develop its own very large airliner, designated A3XX. Airbus considered several designs, including an unusual side-by-side combination of two fuselages from its A340, the largest Airbus jet at the time. In July 1995, the joint study with Boeing was abandoned, as Boeing's interest had declined due to analysis that such a product was unlikely to cover the projected $15 billion development cost. Boeing went on to study a concept known as the New Large Airplane (NLA), an all-new four-engine 500-seat plus successor to the 747, but this too was abandoned in favour of stretched versions of its well-proven 747 series.

In Europe, the A3XX project soon had to face a series of unexpected problems that affected sales projections, the worst of which was a financial crisis that enveloped East Asia in 1997. Airbus took the step of modifying its A3XX design from a single-deck layout to a double-deck configuration, allowing for the carriage of more passengers and aiming for a reduction of 15–20 percent in operating costs compared to those of the existing Boeing 747-400.

The double-deck configuration selected for the A380 was by no means unique. It had already been used in the design of the Boeing Stratocruiser airliner of the late 1940s, developed from the C-97 military transport, which was itself a derivative of the B-29 Superfortress strategic bomber. Basically, what the Boeing designers did was to take a B-29 fuselage and superimpose a second, larger fuselage on it, creating a double-bubble structure in the form of an inverted figure 8. The formula proved very successful, and although the Stratocruiser's reliability was poor, mainly because of problems with its four 28-cylinder Pratt & Whitney R-4360 Wasp Major radial engines (only 55 aircraft were built for commercial service), the military C-97 went on to see widespread service as a transport and flight refuelling tanker in the USAF.

On 19 December 2000, the supervisory board of the newly restructured Airbus

The Boeing Model 377 Stratocruiser of the 1940s featured a double-hull configuration, clearly defined in this image. (Chalmers Butterfield)

France's postwar aviation industry also produced a double-deck transport, the Breguet 763 Deux-Ponts. The type served in relatively small numbers with Air France and the French Air Force in the 1950s. (Armand Agababian)

voted to launch a €9.5 billion ($10.7 billion) project to build the A3XX, redesignated as the A380, with 50 firm orders from six launch customers. The A380 designation was a break from previous Airbus families which had progressed sequentially from A300 to A340. It was chosen because the number 8 resembles the double-deck cross-section and is a lucky number in some Asian countries where the aircraft was being marketed.

The plan was to offer two variants of the A380: the A380-800 passenger model and the A380F freighter. The A380-800 could be configured to carry 555 passengers in three

The interior of the A380's economy class cabin. (Airbus)

classes, or 853 passengers in a single-class configuration, 530 on the main deck and 315 on the upper deck. The design range of the A380-800 was 8,500 nautical miles, sufficient to fly from Hong Kong to New York nonstop.

Variants

The second variant, the A380F freighter, would have been able to lift 150 tonnes of cargo over a range of 5,600nm (10,400km), but although a few initial orders were placed and a combi version was envisaged, able to carry both freight and passengers, this model was cancelled so that Airbus could give priority to production of the A380-800 passenger version.

Airbus also proposed a 656-seat variant, the A380-200, followed in December 2007 by a further proposal for an even larger development, the A380-900, with a seating capacity for 650 passengers in standard configuration and approximately 900 passengers in economy-only configuration. Airlines that expressed an interest in the A380-900 proposal included Emirates, Virgin Atlantic, Cathay Pacific, Air France, KLM, Lufthansa, Kingfisher Airlines (an airline group based in India) and International Lease Finance Corporation. However, in May 2010 Airbus announced that the A380-900 development would be postponed until production of the A380-800 stabilized.

In 2014 conflicting rumours began to emerge that suggested, on the one hand, that A380 production might be halted before its time because of reduced demand, and on the other, that Airbus was contemplating a stretched version of the airliner offering an additional 50 seats to satisfy the requirements of at least six potential customers. The aircraft would

Airbus unveiled its proposed A380plus at the 2017 Paris Air Show, but the concept failed to attract firm interest among major customers. (Airbus)

possibly feature new engines, most probably developed by Rolls-Royce, and would be designated A380neo (New Engine Option). However, in 2016, following the collapse of talks with Emirates, a potential customer for the A380neo, Airbus announced that the project would not go ahead.

Instead, Airbus proposed an enhanced version of the A380 known as the A380plus, with revamped cabin space to accommodate up to 80 more seats, split scimitar winglets and an increase of four percent in fuel economy. Maximum takeoff weight would be increased to 578 tonnes and range by 300nm. This project also stagnated after potential customers – notably Emirates, who concluded that it had no need for the 11-abreast seating configuration featured in the A380plus – lost interest.

Saving weight

In an aircraft the size of the A380, weight-saving measures in construction were of paramount importance. While most of the airliner's fuselage is made of aluminium alloys, composite materials comprise more than 20 percent of the A380's airframe. Carbon fibre-reinforced plastic, glass fibre-reinforced plastic and quartz fibre-reinforced plastic are used extensively in wings, fuselage sections (such as the undercarriage and rear end), tail surfaces and doors. The A380 is the first commercial airliner to have a central wing box made of carbon fibre-reinforced plastic. It is also the first to have a smoothly contoured wing cross–section. This is a variation from the wings of other airliners which are partitioned into sections along the span. The A380's flowing continuous cross-section reduces aerodynamic drag. Thermoplastics (polymers which have a simple molecular structure comprising

The distinctive gull-wing configuration of the A380 is apparent in this photograph (JetPhjotos/Rainer Spoddig)

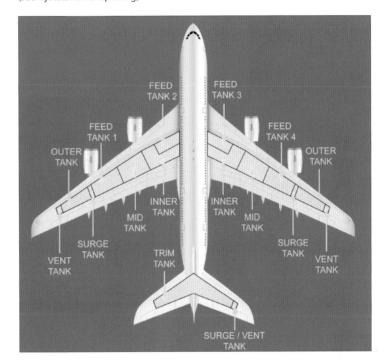

Diagram showing the distribution of the fuel tanks in the A380. (Airbus)

This image provides an excellent view of the A380's landing flaps, spoilers, slats and engine nacelles. (Airbus)

A passenger's view of the flaps and spoilers incorporated in the A380's wing. (Airbus)

chemically independent macromolecules which are softened or melted on heating, then shaped, formed, welded and solidified when cooled) are used in the leading edges of the slats.

A hybrid fibre–metal laminate material known as GLARE (glass laminate aluminium-reinforced epoxy) is used in the upper fuselage and on the stabilizers' leading edges. This aluminium–glass fibre laminate is lighter and has better corrosion and impact resistance than conventional aluminium alloys used in aviation. Unlike earlier composite materials, GLARE can be repaired using conventional aluminium repair techniques.

Weldable aluminium alloys are used in the A380's airframe. This enables the widespread use of laser beam welding manufacturing techniques, eliminating rows of rivets and resulting in a lighter, stronger structure.

It takes 950 US gallons (3,600 litres) of paint to cover the 33,000ft² (3,100m²) exterior of an A380. The paint is five layers thick and weighs about 1,430lb (650kg).

The A380's wings, the largest ever incorporated into a civil airliner design, are designed to cope with a maximum takeoff weight of over 650 tonnes. The wings incorporate wingtip fences that extend above and below the wing surface, similar to those on the A310 and A320. These increase fuel efficiency and range by reducing induced drag. The wingtip fences also reduce wake turbulence, which can endanger following aircraft. Each wing has eight spoilers which come into play to assist the ailerons in assuring roll control at high speeds. The spoilers also act as air brakes, reducing the lift from the wing during the landing phase and ensuring a gentle touchdown by partially extending as soon as the aircraft's sensors detect that contact with the runway has been made by one main wheel, and then extending fully once three main wheels have made contact. The ailerons also have an air brake function on landing, deflecting upwards to 25 degrees.

The A380's wing features both slats and droops to provide lift augmentation at low speeds. Slats are spring-loaded and lie flush with the wing leading edge, held in place by the force of the air acting on them. As the aircraft slows down the aerodynamic force is reduced and the springs extend the slats. Droops, in contrast, are mounted on the rounded leading edge of the wing and the entire leading edge section rotates downwards. The A380 has a droop between the fuselage and each inboard engine, where the leading edge is thickest.

Cockpit systems

The A380 has a cockpit layout and similar procedures to those of other Airbus aircraft, simplifying crew training and reducing costs. Fly-by-wire flight controls are linked to side sticks. The cockpit features eight 5.9x7.9in (15x20cm) liquid crystal displays, comprising two primary flight displays, two navigation displays, one engine parameter display, one system display and two multi-function displays.

The A380's avionics suite has many features originally developed for advanced military aircraft, such as the Lockheed Martin F-22 Raptor, Lockheed Martin F-35 Lightning II and Dassault Rafale, all brought together for an Integrated Modular Avionics (IMA) suite, designed and developed by Airbus, Thales and Diehl Aerospace. The suite is a technological innovation with networked computing modules to support different applications.

The A380's cockpit is paperless, thanks to a Network Systems Server (NSS) that eliminates the need for bulky manuals and documents to be carried. The NSS stores data and offers electronic documentation, providing a required equipment list, navigation charts, performance calculations, and an aircraft logbook. It is accessed through the multi-function displays (MFDs) and controlled via the keyboard interface.

The engines

By 1966, development of the A380 had progressed to such an extent that Rolls-Royce were in a position to announce that the company would proceed with the development of its new Trent 900 engine to power the airliner. In October 2000 Singapore Airlines specified that the Trent 900 would be the power plant for its ten A380s. Qantas followed suit in February 2001. The Trent 900 was air-tested for the first time on 17 May 2004 on Airbus's A340-300 testbed, replacing the aircraft's port inner CFM56 engine. Its final certification was granted by EASA on 29 October 2004 and the FAA on 4 December 2006. Production of the Trent 900 was delayed by a year because of problems with the A380 but was restarted in October 2007, British Airways having announced the previous month that the engine would power the 12 aircraft it had on order.

The Trent 900 series comes in two thrust ratings for the A380: 70,000lb and 72,000lb but is capable of achieving 81,000lb. It features a significant amount of technology inherited from the Trent 8104 demonstrator including its 116in (2.95m) diameter swept-back fan which provides greater thrust for the same engine size and is also about 15 percent lighter than previous wide-chord blades. It is also the first member of the Trent family to feature a contra-rotating HP spool and uses the core of the very reliable Trent 500. It is the only A380 engine that can be transported whole on a Boeing 747 freighter.

The Trent 900 family of engines underwent their first upgrade in 2012. This package, marketed as the Trent 900EP, delivered a one percent saving on fuel burn compared to non-EP engines. A second (EP2) upgrade was based on improvements made during the development of the Trent XWB, intended for the Airbus A350 XWB; these included elliptical leading edges in the compressor, smaller low-pressure turbine tip clearances and new coating for the high-pressure compressor drum, as well as an upgrade to the engine control software. The EP2 package was tested in May 2013 and was available for delivery by May the following year.

The GP7000 alternative

The alternative A380 engine is the Engine Alliance GP7000 turbofan, originally intended to power the cancelled Boeing 747-500X/600X. Engine Alliance was a 50/50 joint venture between General Electric Aircraft Engines and Pratt & Whitney and was formed in August 1996 specifically to develop, manufacture, sell and support a family of modern technology

The Rolls-Royce Trent 900 turbofan, one of the two engine types selected as options for the Airbus A380. (Rolls-Royce)

engines for high-capacity, long-range aircraft. Ground testing of the engine began in April 2004 and was first flight tested as the number two engine on GE's 747 flying testbed over Victorville, CA, in December 2004. Ground testing on the A380 was began at Toulouse on 14 August 2006 on A380-861 MSN009 and the same aircraft took the engine into the air on a four-hour flight ten days later.

Passenger comfort

The key element in marketing the A380-800 was passenger comfort. Firstly, the A380-800's cabin has 5,920 square feet (550 square metres) of usable floor space, 40 percent more than that of the next biggest airliner, the Boeing 747-800. With the aim of reducing passenger fatigue, Airbus introduced measures to make the interior of the aircraft up to 50 percent quieter than that of the Boeing 747-400 and the pressurization more comfortable; the A380-800 is pressurized to an equivalent altitude of 5,000 feet (1,520m) up to 39,000 feet (12,000m).

The A380's upper and lower decks are connected by two stairways, fore and aft, wide enough to accommodate two passengers side by side. This arrangement

The Engine Alliance GP7200 was the preferred engine choice for the Emirates A380 fleet. (Engine Alliance)

The A380 stairway leading from the lower to the upper deck. (Airbus)

Creature comforts on Emirates Airbus A380-861 A6-EDA. A fisheye view of the main bar located at the rear section of the upper deck.
(Kenneth Iwelumo collection)

A luxury cabin in one of Emirates' A380s. (Emirates)

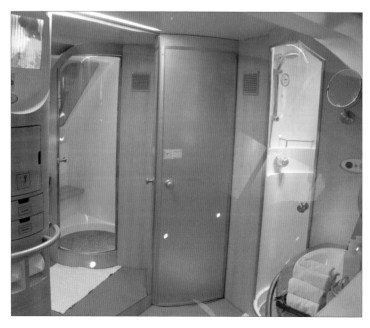

The luxurious first class shower spa in one of Emirates' A380s. (Emirates)

permits multiple seat configurations depending on the customer's requirements. For example, a typical three-class layout of 525 seats accommodates ten first, 76 second and 439 economy class seats. Initial operators typically configured their A380s for three-class service, while adding extra features for passengers in premium cabins. Launch customer Singapore Airlines introduced partly enclosed first class suites on its A380s in 2007, each featuring a leather seat with a separate bed; centre suites could be joined to create a double bed. A year later, Qantas installed a new first class seat-bed and a sofa lounge at the front of the upper deck on its A380s and in 2009 Air France unveiled an upper-deck electronic art gallery. In late 2008 Emirates introduced first class shower spas on its A380s, allowing each first class passenger five minutes of hot water via a tank containing 2.5 tonnes.

The A380 Building Programme

The A380 production programme involved an unprecedented collaborative effort on the part of the constructors, the components being built in the various member countries and then transported by ship, barge, road and air to Toulouse for final assembly.

The United Kingdom had been involved in the Airbus family of widebody airliners from the beginning, although the road had not always been smooth. On 26 September 1967 the British, French, and West German governments signed a memorandum of understanding to start development of the 300-seat Airbus A300, the first of the family. At the time, news of the announcement had been clouded by the British government's support for the Airbus, which coincided with its refusal to back BAC's proposed competitor, the British Aircraft Company (BAC) 2–11, despite a preference for the latter expressed by British European Airways. (BEA). In 1969 the British government announced that it would withdraw its support for the Airbus project. The Managing Director of Hawker Siddeley decided that his company would remain in the project as a favoured sub-contractor developing and manufacturing the wings for the A300, which would become pivotal in later versions' impressive performance from short domestic to long intercontinental flights. Hawker Siddeley spent £35 million of its own funds, along with a further £35 million loan from the West German government, on the machine tooling to design and produce the wings.

At this time, Hawker Siddeley was the acknowledged leader in the design of advanced airliner wings, having amassed a huge volume of experience with its Trident airliner, whose wing was the most aerodynamically advanced of any airliner's. In 1977 Hawker Siddeley merged with the BAC to form British Aerospace (BAe), which rejoined the Airbus consortium in 1979 as a full member, responsible for the design and manufacture of wings for all Airbus models.

In the United Kingdom the A380's wings were designed and built at two sites: Filton, near Bristol and Broughton, North Wales. Filton was selected as the base for the multinational integrated wing-design team and the aircraft component management

teams for both the A380 wing and landing gear. The Filton site also featured a rib manufacturing facility, where 40 of the 124 composite wing ribs in an A380 wing-set were manufactured.

Broughton is the ultimate destination for the 32,000 components which comprise a set of A380 wings. These components and sub-assemblies are assembled into a complete wingbox – measuring over 45 metres along the leading edge for the A380. The wingboxes are then equipped with more components, including the installation of fuel, pneumatic and hydraulic systems and wiring. The Broughton factory covers an area of 83,500 square metres and is more than 1,310 feet (400m) long and 656 feet

Top: The Airbus facility at Filton, near Bristol. (Airbus UK)

Above: A section of the A380's massive wing in production at Broughton. (Airbus UK)

A view inside the Airbus facility at Broughton. (Airbus UK)

An A380 being assembled at Toulouse. (Airbus)

(200m) wide, with a maximum height of 115 feet (35m).

The centre wing box and front section of the fuselage are built in France. Several major components of the A380 are manufactured and assembled at Airbus sites in Nantes, St Nazaire and Méaulte, prior to final assembly on the assembly line at Toulouse.

In Nantes, a 107,640ft^2 (10,000m^2) workshop houses the manufacture and assembly of the centre wing box, the first to be made from carbon fibre-reinforced plastic, regarded to be one of the innovative features of the A380. At St Nazaire the fuselage assembly hall was increased by some 53,820ft^2 (5,000m^2) to assemble, equip and test the forward and centre section of the A380 fuselage. The central fuselage alone comprises five separate large components, including the centre wing box and landing gear bays which are manufactured at Nantes and the Airbus site at Méaulte. A laser-based measuring system ensures that the components are fitted together with maximum accuracy.

Germany manufactures the A380's fuselage and vertical tail unit, which are built and assembled at the Nordenham, Stade and Hamburg sites in northern Germany. The fuselage shells are produced in Nordenham and are then shipped to Hamburg in large, special containers using a roll-on-roll-off system.

Once in Hamburg, the fuselage shells are assembled in the major component assembly hall. The Hamburg plant delivers three A380 fuselage sections: the forward section behind the cockpit, the rear fuselage section and the upper half of the fuselage shell above the wings, which is transported to Saint-Nazaire for further assembly. At the Stade composite site the vertical tail fin for the A380 is manufactured as well as landing flaps shells and pressure bulkheads.

Spain is responsible for the tailplane (also known as the horizontal stabilizer), the rear fuselage tail cone and the belly fairing for the A380. The tailplane is manufactured at Getafe, in the Madrid region, and the other fuselage components at Illescas (Toledo).

Final assembly and functional testing of the tailplane is carried out at Puerto Real, in the Cadiz region. This plant is also responsible for producing the tailplane's lateral boxes for the A350 XWB and A330 families, and elevators for the A320 family.

After shipment of all the A380 components to Toulouse, all sections are moved into position on the jigs in the main assembly hall for final assembly. When all the parts are in position a 1,200-tonne jig, with five levels and four lifts to facilitate access, envelops the aircraft. The three sections of fuselage are joined together and the wings joined to the complete fuselage after being moved into position, first by overhead cranes and then laser alignment. It takes around 4,000 rivets to join one wing to the fuselage.

Usually, when the average production rate reached a peak of four aircraft per month, the fully assembled A380 airframe remained in the final assembly station for one week before being moved out of the hall through its vast 90-metre-wide sliding doors into the adjacent hall where there is room for three A380s to have their systems completed and tested. The engines are also fitted at this location.

Over the following weeks a series of very extensive tests are conducted to ensure that all electrical and hydraulic systems, as well as all moving parts such as the rudder, spoilers and elevators, are in full working order. As with all Airbus models, all sections are fully tested, checked and controlled at their respective production sites. The purpose of the checks on the final assembly line is to ensure that all parts work well together. Once these final controls are completed, the aircraft is moved outside to have its cabin tested. Air is pumped into the cabin to increase pressure to a level far beyond what the aircraft will be subjected to in service to test for leakages.

Once all tests have been completed, the aircraft is handed over to the Flight Test Department to be prepared for its first flight.

An Airbus A380 for Lufthansa taking shape in the Airbus factory (Baustelle 1) at Hamburg. (Airbus)

Aerial view of the A380 construction facility at Hamburg. (Airbus)

A fuselage section of the second A380, MSN002 F-WXXL, being transported by road. This aircraft was retained by Airbus for flight trials. (Airbus)

An Airbus A380 pictured at Getafe, Spain, where the Airbus facility manufactures the airliner's tailplane. (Airbus)

A transporter carrying the rear fuselage section of an Airbus threads its way along the street of a French town. Although this component does not belong to an A380, the photograph well illustrates the difficulty attending road transport. (Airbus)

Transporting A380 components by road requires the use of equally massive land vehicles, as seen here. (Airbus)

The *City of Hamburg* was one of three roll-on/roll-off (RORO) vessels used to transport Airbus A380 components by sea. (Airbus)

A Super Guppy operated by NASA is pictured at the moment of touchdown. (NASA)

Support infrastructure

Building the A380 involved the creation of a massive support infrastructure, as the large size of the various sections made traditional transportation methods impracticable. For the surface movement of large A380 structural components a complex route known as the *Itinéraire à Grand Gabarit* was developed. This involved the construction of a fleet of roll-on/roll-off (RORO) ships and barges, the construction of port facilities and the development of new and modified roads to accommodate oversized road convoys. The front and rear fuselage sections are shipped on one of three RORO ships from Hamburg in northern Germany to Saint-Nazaire in France. The ship travels via Mostyn in the United Kingdom, where the wings – manufactured at Broughton in North Wales – are transported by barge to Mostyn docks and loaded for sea transport. In Saint-Nazaire, the ship exchanges the fuselage sections from Hamburg for larger, assembled sections, some of which include the nose. The ship unloads in Bordeaux and then proceeds to Cadiz in southern Spain, where it picks up the belly and tail sections from Construcciones Aeronauticas SA (CASA) and delivers them to Bordeaux. From there, the A380 parts are transported by barge to Langon, and by oversize road convoys to the Jean-Luc Lagardere assembly hall in Toulouse. To avoid damage from direct handling, parts are secured in custom jigs carried on self-powered wheeled vehicles. After assembly the aircraft are flown to Hamburg Finkenwerder Airport to be fitted out and painted.

When Airbus started in 1970 road vehicles were initially used for the movement of all components and sections of its various aircraft. However, growth in production volume soon necessitated a switch to air transport. From 1972 onwards a fleet of four highly modified transport aircraft, known as Super Guppies were brought into service. These were former Boeing Stratocruisers that had been converted with custom fuselages and fitted with turboprop engines. They had previously been used by NASA to transport high-volume loads in support of the US space programme. As time went on, the Super Guppies grew increasingly unsatisfactory for Airbus's ferrying needs. Their age meant that operating expenses were high and ever-increasing, and growing Airbus production required greater capacity than could be provided by the existing fleet.

Various options were studied to serve as a replacement transport medium for the Super Guppies, including methods of surface transportation by road, rail, and sea. These alternatives were discarded in favour of a principally air-based solution as they were considered to have reliability concerns and were time-consuming in operation. In addition, the assembly line in Toulouse was not conveniently accessible by any of the surface methods. A

Construction of the first Airbus Beluga, based on the Airbus A300, with an oversized cargo compartment on top, started in September 1992. The first of five aircraft flew in September 1994. (Airbus)

key requirement of the new air transporter was the need to accommodate every major component being manufactured by Airbus, including the then-heaviest planned part, the wing of the larger variants of the Airbus A340. A speedy development programme was also necessitated in order to begin introducing the prospective type in time to take over duties from the Super Guppy fleet, which was scheduled to draw down in the mid-1990s.

Several different types of large transport aircraft were considered, but the use of any existing aircraft was eventually discounted due to a lack of internal space to accommodate the desired components. The use of a piggyback arrangement was also dismissed as impractical. Boeing made their own offer to convert several Boeing 767s for the requirement, but this was viewed as inferior to developing a purpose-built aircraft using Airbus's existing widebody twin-engined Airbus A300-600R instead.

In September 1992 construction work began on the first aircraft, the maiden flight of which took place in September 1994. Following a total of 335 flight hours performed during the test programme, restricted certification of the type was awarded by the European Aviation Safety Agency (EASA) in October 1995, enabling the A300-600ST Beluga to enter service shortly thereafter. In addition to the first aircraft, four more Belugas were constructed at a rate of roughly one per year. From start to finish each airframe reportedly took roughly three years to complete. Modification work was performed at Toulouse using components provided by the Airbus assembly line. Originally, a total of four aircraft were to be built along with an option for a fifth being available, which was later firmed up.

The fleet's primary task is to carry Airbus components ready for final assembly across Europe between Toulouse, Hamburg and nine other sites, and they do so 60 times a week. The Beluga fleet is owned by Airbus Transport International (ATI), a wholly owned subsidiary of Airbus Group that was established specifically to operate the type. Through this organization the fleet is made available for hire by third parties for charter flight. Over time the Beluga has been used to carry a variety of special loads, including space station components, large and delicate artwork, industrial machinery and intact helicopters. The A300-600ST's freight compartment is 24 feet (7.4m) in diameter and 124 feet (37.7m) long, with a maximum payload of 47 tonnes.

Flying the A380

Five A380s were built for testing and demonstration purposes. The first A380, MSN001, registered F-WWOW, was unveiled in Toulouse on 18 January 2005. This aircraft spent three months on the A380 final assembly line at Toulouse having all its essential systems fully tested, including its hydraulics, landing gear and electrics. Safety tests were also made at this point on the fuel pipes to check for leaks and ensure the system was operating correctly. Another A380 airframe, MSN5000, and in fact the first to be assembled, was used for static testing; this airframe would never fly and was not equipped with hydraulics and avionics. It was subjected to a series of rigorous structural tests designed to feed back aircraft loading data to the flight test team before the first flight of MSN001. These tests were carried out in a purpose-built building next to the assembly line and were undertaken by the Centre d'essais Aéronautiques. The static test programme lasted nine weeks and included tests to establish how the aircraft's wings and whole fuselage behaved when subjected to both normal and exceptional loads, such as might be encountered during flight in extremely rare circumstances. Once the initial phase was complete the team began a year-long certification test programme, looking at how the aircraft resists ultra-high loads under a wide range of flying and rolling conditions. Post-certification, a series of tests were run to load the aircraft's fuselage and wings until they broke. These tests allowed engineers to check that the ruptures occur where predicted. On 14 February 2006, during the destructive-wing-strength certification test on MSN5000, the test wing of the A380 failed at 145 percent of the limit load, short of the required 150 percent level. Airbus announced modifications adding 66lb (30kg) to the wing to provide the required strength. On 26 March 2006, the A380 underwent evacuation certification in Hamburg. With eight of the 16 exits arbitrarily blocked, 853 mixed passengers and 20 crew exited the darkened aircraft in 78 seconds, less than the 90 seconds required for certification. Three days later, the A380 received EASA and United States FAA approval to carry up to 853 passengers.

A second static A380 airframe to come off the line, MSN5001, underwent four weeks of fatigue testing, essential for the first flight clearance and certification programme. Around 900 acceleration sensors were installed on the aircraft's lifting surfaces, decks, engines, systems and landing gears. More than 20 exciters forced the structure to vibrate so that the way it responded could be closely monitored. These tests were undertaken at Dresden and on their completion, the airframe was broken up and the centre section shipped to Toulouse.

The A380 takes to the sky

The first A380 to fly, on 27 April 2005, was MSN001, registered F-WWOW. This aircraft, equipped with Rolls-Royce Trent 900 engines, flew from Toulouse-Blagnac Airport with a crew of six, headed by chief test pilot Jacques Rosay, who afterwards said flying the A380 had been 'like handling a bicycle'.

F-WWOW was retained by Airbus and used as a Rolls-Royce engine testbed.

On 1 December 2005, the A380 achieved its maximum design speed of Mach 0.96, (its design cruise speed is Mach 0.85) in a shallow dive. In 2006, the A380 flew its first high-altitude test at Addis Ababa Bole Airport. It conducted its second high-altitude test at the same airport in 2009. On 10 January 2006 it flew to José Maria Cordova International Airport in Colombia, accomplishing the transatlantic testing, and then went to El Dorado International Airport to test the engine operation in high-altitude airports. It arrived in North America on 6 February 2006, landing at Iqualuit, Nunavut in Canada for cold-weather testing.

Somewhat confusingly, the second A380 to fly was MSN004 F-WWDD, the fourth on the production line, which was also

A composite photograph showing an A380 wing section undergoing extreme testing at the Dresden facility. (Airbus)

Left: The cockpit of the A380. (Airbus)

Below: The flight test engineer's station on the lower deck of the first A380 to fly, F-WWOW. (Airbus)

retained by Airbus for use as the Engine Alliance GP7200 engine testbed. The second aircraft, MSN 002 F-WXXL, was also retained by Airbus for various flight trials; it was originally to have been purchased for private use by a member of the Saudi royal family, Prince Alwaleed bin Talal, but the order was cancelled. The aircraft eventually ended up in the Aeroscopia aviation museum at Toulouse-Blagnac.

The first A380 using GP7200 engines – serial number MSN009 and registration F-WWEA – flew on 25 August 2006. On 4 September 2006 the first full passenger-carrying flight test took place. The aircraft flew from Toulouse with 474 Airbus employees on board, in a test of passenger facilities and comfort. In November 2006 a further series of route-proving flights demonstrated the aircraft's performance for 150 flight hours under typical airline operating conditions. As of 2014, the A380 test aircraft continue to perform test procedures.

Airbus obtained type certificates for the A380-841 and A380-842 model from EASA and FAA on 12 December 2006 in a joint ceremony at the company's French headquarters, receiving the ICAO code A388. The A380-861 model was added to the type certificate on 14 December 2007.

Takeoff and cruise
As part of the pre-takeoff procedure, the A380's flight crew first inputs data relevant to the departure airport, such as runway in use, which intersection will be used, takeoff run, possible obstacles, emergency runway exits in the event of an engine failure on takeoff and so on. Other inputs include data on the prevailing conditions, such as wind direction and speed, outside air temperature, pressure above sea level (QNH), runway conditions and possible icing conditions. The latter is defined as when the outside air temperature on the

ground and in flight is 10°C or below and visible moisture in any form is present, such as clouds, fog reducing visibility to one nautical mile or less, rain, snow, sleet or ice crystals. The presence of standing water, snow, ice or slush on the runway must also be taken into account.

The upper deck of the A380, equipped with water-filled ballast tanks during the flight-test phase. (Airbus)

One critical value that must be entered into the system is the aircraft's weight on takeoff, on which depends such factors as the flap setting and power setting. Unless the aircraft is taking off at maximum weight, when maximum thrust would be required, takeoff is usually achieved with less than maximum power, which depends on the outside air temperature. As the latter increases, the air density decreases, reducing the amount of power the engines produce. The A380's system takes all the parameters into account and calculates the amount of thrust required for safe takeoff.

With all the cockpit and systems checks completed, the A380 is taxied out and lined up on the runway, where the pre-takeoff checks are carried out. All four thrust levers are moved forward until about 30 percent thrust is reached. The A380 is fitted with a thrust system called Airbus Cockpit Universal Acute Emulator (ACUTE), which shows how much thrust the engines are producing as a percentage of the maximum.

With the flaps set to the appropriate value, depending on the required takeoff speed and the desired rate of climb after takeoff, the thrust levers are advanced beyond the 30 percent level, the system tells the engines to accelerate to the level previously calculated and the aircraft begins its takeoff roll. The handling pilot ensures that the A380 tracks correctly down the runway centreline using the rudder pedals to make small adjustments while the second (non-handling) pilot monitors the systems. When the appropriate rotation speed is reached, the pilot gently pulls back on the side stick and the nose lifts, the airliner rotates at about three degrees per second until it achieves a climb-out attitude of 12.5 degrees. With all 20 main wheels and two nose wheels successfully retracted, the pilot lowers the nose at 1,000 feet, reduces the thrust, retracts the flaps and the aircraft accelerates to the usual climb speed of 250 knots below 10,000 feet, increasing to 330 knots above that altitude.

Cruising altitude

Like most other commercial aircraft, the Airbus A380 typically cruises at 35,000 feet, the altitude where the air is thin enough to reduce drag, thereby increasing fuel efficiency and lowering operating costs, but also retaining enough oxygen to feed the engines. Also, most of the earth's weather occurs in the troposphere, the layer of the atmosphere which is closest to the ground and extends up to about 36,000 feet. Flying at the top of this layer avoids flying through all but the most extreme weather conditions, reduces the possibility of encountering flocks of birds and keeps the aircraft well above the normal cruising altitude of light aircraft and helicopters. The maximum certified cruise altitude for the A380 is 43,000 feet.

Descent and landing

The landing characteristics of the A380 are similar to those of earlier members of the Airbus family, despite the A380's massive size. Letdown starts at approximately 0.85 Mach at cruise altitude, the pilots having entered relevant data such as surface winds into the flight management system. As it passes 10,000 feet in the descent, the aircraft is slowed to 250 knots and generally enters the landing pattern at 180 knots. Pilots are able to control the rate of descent and speed manually using knobs on the autopilot control panel, allowing the flight management system to do the work. The design of the A380's wings, with their large area, comparatively gentle sweep of 33.5 degrees, and massive flaps, give the

The Mighty A380 in landing configuration, with everything down! (Airbus)

aircraft a landing speed some 20 knots lower than that of a Boeing 747. The A380 crosses the runway threshold at 140 knots and touches down at 130 knots.

The A380's braking system is manufactured by Honeywell Aerospace, a hugely experienced company that has been designing and building such systems for both civil and military aircraft since the Second World War. The composite, anti-skid brakes are fixed to 16 of the aircraft's 20 main landing gear wheels. The brakes were rigorously tested during the trials phase, when the aircraft was loaded to its maximum takeoff weight and launched down the runway until it reached 170 knots, the decision speed at which the pilot would either elect to continue or abort the takeoff. The pilot then retarded the throttles and stood on the brakes, bringing the A380 to a stop in 6,070 feet (1,850m). Also crucial to the landing roll are 16 spoilers which deploy upwards from the wing to create drag and reduce lift.

Most modern airliners use reversers that redirect engine thrust forward. On many turbofan engines the airflow bypassing the engine core is blocked from exiting (though the combustion exhaust is not) and is channelled through an assembly of vanes (a cascade) exposed when an outer sleeve on the engine nacelle slides aft. Airliners are not required to have thrust reversers and only the two inboard engines on the A380 are equipped with them. The decision not to install reversers on the A380's two outboard engines saved weight and lowered the chances that those engines, which sometimes hang over runway edges, would be damaged by ingesting foreign objects.

The two reversers do help slow the A380, but not by much. In fact, unlike the thrust reversers on most airliners, including the Boeing 747, they do not stop the aircraft in a shorter distance than brakes and spoilers alone. They do, however, take some of the strain off the brakes and are useful if water or snow makes the runway slippery. On the A380, a pilot can deploy the thrust reversers only on the ground, and can select a range of thrust reversal from idle to maximum reverse, until the aircraft has slowed to below 70 knots, or 80.5mph (one knot equals 1.15mph). At that point, the thrust reversers must be set at idle reverse.

All airliner engines now have safeguards built in to keep the thrust reversers from accidentally deploying during flight. In 1991 a Boeing 767 crashed 15 minutes after taking off from Indonesia, killing all 313 on board, because the thrust reverser on one of its engines deployed at 24,000 feet, sending the aircraft into a high-speed descent. The FAA responded by requiring redundant locks on the equipment. In case of future accidental deployments, in spite of the locks, the agency required new training procedures for cockpit crews to prevent deployment from causing a crash. In 1998 a thrust reverser on a Korean Air Airbus A300 deployed for a few seconds in flight; the crew managed to disable the reverser and land safely.

Trials and tribulations

Inevitably, the development and testing of every new aircraft reveals a succession of snags. In the case of the A380 the snags were bigger than most, causing delays that were to have a serious effect on the airliner's production schedule.

The biggest problem involved the A380's electrical system, or, to be precise, the complex system of wiring that had to be treated through the various sections of the airframe. The airliner's electrical system required 330 miles (530km) of wiring, cables and wiring harnesses, with more

The A380's 20-wheel main undercarriage unit. (Airbus/Florian Lindner)

The wiring system installed in the upper deck of the A380. (Airbus)

The complex nature of the wiring installation of the A380 is apparent in this image. (Airbus)

The wiring system in the main deck ceiling of the A380. (Airbus)

than 100,000 wires and 40,000 connectors performing 1,150 separate functions. It was by far the most complex electrical system ever designed by Airbus, and trouble arose even as the prototype A380, F-WWOW, was being built at Toulouse. Although the electrical wires and their harnesses had been manufactured in accordance with the specification and should, in theory, have been installed without any problem, in practice they turned out to be too short. An analysis of the problem revealed that the different design groups working on the project had used different Computer-Aided Design (CAD) software to create the engineering drawings. These groups were spread across 16 separate sites in the four partner companies. While German and Spanish designers had used one version of the software, the British and French teams had used an upgraded version. Without going into complex technical detail, this led to incorrect calculations that affected the wiring as it wound its way through the airframe, especially at the points where it had to be bent around structural components.

The result was that the wiring had to be stripped out of the prototype, redesigned, new harnesses manufactured and the wing threaded back through the airframe. It was a monumental task involving hundreds of engineers. In the end it all boiled down to the fact that the decision to proceed with the project before the CAD systems were fully integrated should never have been taken. Eventually the A380 emerged as a very fine aircraft indeed, and Airbus attained a new level of integration and cooperation, but only after billons of dollars had been lost and customer confidence shaken to its core.

Customers

The launch customer for the A380 was Singapore Airlines, which announced an order for up to 25 Airbus A3XXs (as the A380 was known at the time) on 29 September 2000. The deal, costing $8.6 billion, involved a firm order for ten aircraft, with options on 15 more airframes. The order was confirmed by Singapore Airlines on 12 July 2001, and in January 2005 the airline unveiled the slogan 'First to Fly the A380 – Experience the Difference in 2006' to promote the anticipated delivery of its first A380-800 in the second quarter of 2006. However, in June 2005 Airbus confirmed that due to unforeseen technical problems, initial deliveries of the A380 would be delayed by up to six months, an announcement that prompted SIA's chief executive officer to state that the airline would turn its attention to Boeing instead, since it would be receiving the Boeing 777-300ER before the A380. He also threatened to sue Airbus. Nevertheless, the A380 promotional campaign went ahead and in February 2006 the first A380, in full Singapore Airlines livery, was flown to Singapore where it went on display at Asian Aerospace 2006.

On 14 June 2006 Singapore Airlines placed an initial order for the Boeing 787 Dreamliner as part of its future aircraft expansion programme. The order consisted of 20 787-9s with an option on 20 more. The order was placed a day after Airbus revealed that delivery of the A380 would be delayed by a further six months. A third delay was announced on 3 October 2006, pushing back delivery of the first A380 to October 2007.

Singapore Airlines finally took delivery of its first aircraft (9V-SKA) on 15 October 2007. Route flying with this aircraft began on 25 October 2007, with flight number SQ380 operating between Singapore and Sydney. The 455 passengers on this inaugural flight were able to buy seats in a charity online auction, paying between $560 and $100,380. The airline donated all revenue generated from the flight to three charities in a ceremony the next day in Sydney. SIA began regular services with the A380 on 28 October 2007. Two months later, Singapore Airlines CEO Chew Choong Seng stated the A380 was performing better than either the airline or Airbus had anticipated, burning 20 percent less fuel per seat-mile than the airline's 747-400 fleet.

In 2016 the airline confirmed that one A380 would be returned to its leasing company at the end of its ten-year lease in October 2017, with a decision still to be made regarding retention of four additional A380 aircraft whose leases were due to expire between January and June 2018.

Above: A Singapore Airlines A380 sits on the wet tarmac at Singapore Changi Airport, awaiting the fitting of a replacement engine. (SIA)

Left: A Singapore Airlines A380 pictured at the moment of takeoff. (Airbus)

Right: A dramatic shot of an Emirates A380 emerging from cloud on its landing approach. (Airbus)

Below: Rollout of the first A380 for Emirates. By far the biggest customer for the A380, Emirates took delivery of its first aircraft in July 2008.

In 2019 Singapore Airlines had 19 A380s in service, with no plans to retire any of them. The A380 fleet was undergoing a series of passenger cabin refits at the time of writing, a somewhat lengthy and complex process.

The second airline to receive the A380, and by far the biggest customer for the airliner, was Emirates, which by the early 1990s had become one of the world's fastest growing airlines, with revenue increasing by approximately US$100 million a year. The Gulf War of 1991 had an impact on the airline's services for a time, but in 1993 Emirates established a partnership with US Airways and began to offer round-the-world services. By 1995, the airline had expanded the fleet to six Airbus A300s and eight Airbus A310s and had built its network up to cover 37 destinations in 30 countries. In 1996 the airline received its first Boeing 777–200 aircraft, followed shortly thereafter by six Boeing 777-200ERs. The arrival of the 777s allowed Emirates to continue its Singapore service

onward to Melbourne commencing in 1996. The flight briefly operated as a Dubai–Jakarta–Melbourne service before being cut due to unprofitability; Emirates would only begin serving Jakarta nonstop again in 2006 when it became a very profitable route for Emirates and would see new destinations added in Australia.

In April 2000 Emirates announced an order for the Airbus A3XX (as mentioned, later named Airbus A380). The deal consisted of five A380-800 passenger aircraft and two freighter versions. The deal was confirmed on 4 November 2001 when Emirates announced orders for 15 more A380-800s. An additional order for 21 A380-800s was placed two years later. In April 2006 Emirates replaced its order for the two freighter variants with an order for two A380-800s. In 2007 Emirates ordered 15 A380-800s, bringing the total ordered to fifty-eight.

The airline took delivery of its first aircraft on 28 July 2008 – the deliveries had been delayed three times by the same set of circumstances that had affected the deliveries to Singapore International Airlines – and began a commercial A380 service between Dubai and New York the following month. The eventual Emirates A380 order rose to 142 aircraft, the 100th aircraft joining the fleet in October 2017. Then, in February 2019, following a review of its operations, Emirates cancelled most of the A380s it still had on order, cutting the number left to be delivered to just fourteen.

The second Middle Eastern airline to place an order for the A380 was Etihad Airways, the flag carrier airline of Abu Dhabi, United Arab Emirates, which began operations in November 2003. Etihad announced an order for four A380s on

Left and below: Etihad Airways took delivery of its first Airbus A380 in July 2014, inaugural services beginning in December. (Etihad)

20 July 2004, which was increased to ten in July 2008, with options on a further five. The aircraft were all to be powered by the Engine Alliance GP7200. The first commercial flight by an Etihad A380 took place on 27 December 2014 when A6-APA flew from Abu Dhabi to London Heathrow.

A third Middle Eastern airline, Qatar Airways, announced an order for two A380s at the Dubai Air Show in January 2004; the order was later increased to ten. The first aircraft, A7-APA, named *Athba*, was delivered on 18 September 2014 and made its first commercial flight from Doha to London Heathrow on 10 October that year.

Qantas, the Australian national carrier, placed an order for 12 A380-800s, beginning passenger services between Melbourne and Los Angeles in October 2008. By the end of the year the A380s had carried 890,000 passengers on 2,200 flights over five major routes, totalling 21,000 flying hours. The Qantas A380 fleet later underwent a substantial refurbishment programme, the first aircraft being returned to service

in October 2019. The upper deck of the refurbished aircraft is entirely comprised of business and premium economy seats, as well as the expanded on-board lounge, while first class and economy class seats are all on the lower deck. Premium seating has increased by 27 percent on the

Qatar Airways A380 A7-APE pictured at London Heathrow. (John Taggart)

upgraded aircraft. The airline introduced the Qantas business suite, replacing its previous Skybed business class seats. The new seats are arranged in a 1-2-1 configuration that now gives aisle access to every passenger. The upgraded aircraft features 70 business suites, six more compared to the older aircraft. The new business seats retain the same 80-inch bed length as the previous model, while the bed width is 24 inches. According to Qantas's own publicity material, the seat can be in the recline position from takeoff right through to landing.

The first reconfigured aircraft, VH-OQK, operated as QF2 from London to Sydney via Singapore. It departed on 1 October 2019 and arrived in Australia on 2 October. Qantas was planning to complete the refurbishment programme by the end of 2020, each aircraft taking about eight weeks to upgrade.

Early in its service with Qantas, the A380 was involved in an incident which generated much alarm and adverse publicity for Rolls-Royce. On 4 November 2010, Qantas Flight 32, on a scheduled passenger service from London to Sydney via Singapore, suffered an uncontained engine failure in one of its Rolls-Royce Trent 900 engines four minutes after takeoff from Singapore Changi Airport. There were no injuries to the passengers, crew or people on the ground, although some debris fell on the Indonesian island of Batam. Qantas grounded all of its A380s that day subject to an internal investigation taken in conjunction with the engine manufacturer. A380s powered by Engine Alliance GP7000 were unaffected, but operators of the A380 powered by the Roll-Royce engines were understandably concerned. Investigators determined that an oil leak, caused by a defective oil supply pipe, led to an engine fire and subsequent uncontained engine failure following the disintegration of a turbine disc in the aircraft's number two engine (on the port side nearest the fuselage), causing extensive damage to the engine nacelle, wing, fuel system, landing gear, flight controls and engine controls. Repairs cost an estimated A\$139 million (US\$145m). As other Rolls-Royce Trent

900 engines also showed problems with the same oil leak, Rolls-Royce ordered many engines to be changed, including about half of the engines in the Qantas A380 fleet. During the aeroplane's repair, cracks were discovered in wing structural fittings which also resulted in mandatory inspections of all A380s and subsequent design changes.

The first European airline to operate the A380 was Air France, which ordered 12 A380-800 aircraft in 2001, with options on two more. The first aircraft was delivered on 30 October 2009, the inaugural route being Paris–New York. In 2018 it was announced that Air France would retire 50 percent of its A380 fleet due to the high cost of operating the aircraft. It would be replacing them with Airbus A350-900s and Boeing 787 Dreamliners. Air France is only retiring the five aircraft that were leased to it by not renewing their leases and returning them directly to Airbus. The five Airbus A380 aircraft bought by Air France will continue service from 2020 onwards with renewed cabins. In August 2019, Air France–KLM revised retirement plans on the Airbus A380 and announced that the entire Airbus A380 fleet would be retired by 2022.

It was an Air France A380 that experienced the second incident involving an engine failure. In this case the engine was an Engine Alliance GP7270. On 30 September 2017 Air France Flight 66, an A380 registration F-HPJE, flying from Paris Charles de Gaulle Airport to Los Angeles International Airport, suffered an apparent uncontained engine failure in its number four engine while flying over Greenland. The aircraft, carrying 497 passengers and 24 crew, successfully diverted to CFB Goose Bay, a military airfield also used by civilian air traffic. As Goose Bay did not have the facilities to accommodate large numbers of passengers from a commercial aircraft, those aboard Flight 66 were asked to remain on board the A380 until the next morning when an Air France Boeing 777 and a chartered Boeing 737 arrived to take them on to their destination. On 6 December 2017 the A380 was ferried from Goose Bay to Charles de Gaulle under the power of its three serviceable engines, and after being fitted with a replacement engine, it was returned to service on 15 January 2018.

As for the incident itself, the first indication was that the engine's fan hub had become detached during the flight and dragged the air intake with it. The FAA acted quickly and released an emergency airworthiness directive (EAD) on 12 October, reporting that an Engine Alliance GP7270 engine had suffered an uncontained engine failure. The report stated that the engine had accumulated 3,527 flight cycles, adding that this was a relatively high engine cycle. The report concluded that the FAA directive had been issued 'to prevent failure of the fan hub, which could lead to uncontained release of the fan hub, damage

The substantial damage sustained by the number two engine of Qantas Flight 32's A380 following an engine fire on 4 November 2010. (Qantas)

to the engine and damage to the airplane. The EAD requires visual inspections of the fan hubs with 3,500 flight cycles or more within 2 weeks and fan hubs with 2,000 or more flight cycles within 8 weeks. The fan hubs are to be removed from service if damage or defects are found outside serviceable limits'.

Some six days after the incident, following an extensive search, debris from the aircraft's engine was recovered in Greenland. France's Air Accident Investigation Agency (BEA) stated that 'the recovery of the missing parts, especially of the fan hub fragments, was the key to supporting the investigation' and initiated a full-scale search that included a widespread operation by a Dassault Falcon 20 aircraft equipped with synthetic aperture radar, but it was not until June 2019 that a major missing piece of the engine weighing 150kg was located on the Greenland ice sheet, buried under the snow, and recovered.

Hard on Air France's heels as an A380 customer was the German airline Lufthansa, which on 6 December 2001 announced an order for 15 aircraft with

The shredded engine nacelle and missing fan hub of Air France Flight 66. (Air France)

Lufthansa Airbus A380-800 D-AIMG approaching to land at Hong Kong International Airport. (Lufthansa)

One of Lufthansa's fleet of A380s, named *Wien* (Vienna), in formation with a pair of Austrian Air Force Saab JAS 39 Gripen fighters. (Lufthansa)

A Lufthansa A380 approaching to land, with one of the airline's fleet of Boeing 747s taxiing in the foreground. (Lufthansa)

ten more options. The aircraft were to be used exclusively for long-haul flights from Frankfurt. The first A380-800 was delivered on 19 May 2010. On 11 June the airline launched an inaugural A380 service between Frankfurt and Tokyo. In September 2011 the order was increased by two more aircraft to seventeen. This order was confirmed on 14 March 2013. However, in September 2013 it was announced that the Lufthansa Supervisory Board had approved the purchase of only 12 of the first 15 A380s, so that 14 A380s have been added to the fleet.

Lufthansa uses its A380s to and from Frankfurt am Main (nine aircraft) and since March 2018 to and from Munich as well (five aircraft). From 6 to 12 December 2011 Lufthansa had already operated an A380 once a day on the route from Munich to New York JFK to accommodate the needs of customers eager to visit New York City for their Christmas shopping. On 13 March 2019 Lufthansa announced that it would be selling six A380 aircraft and replacing them with 20 Boeing 787-9 Dreamliners and 20 Airbus A350-900 aircraft.

In Asia, the market for the A380 appeared healthy, with Korean Air introducing the first of ten aircraft into service on 17 June 2011. In October, China Southern Airlines became the only Chinese airline to order the A380, acquiring five aircraft which were initially operated on the Beijing–Guangzhou and Beijing–Hong Kong routes. However, these services struggled to be profitable,

Korean Air's A380 made its first commercial flight between Incheon International Airport, Seoul, and Narita International Airport, Tokyo, on 17 June 2011. (Korean Air)

A China Southern Airlines Airbus A380 seen at Beijing International Airport. (China Southern)

Above: Malaysia Airlines A380 9M-MNA receiving a pushback at London Heathrow. (MAL)

Left: The first Airbus A380 delivered to Thai Airways is pictured in the airline's colourful livery on the tarmac at Toulouse. (Airbus)

and so the airline started to operate its A380s on the Guangzhou–Los Angeles and Guangzhou–Sydney routes, adding the Beijing–Amsterdam route in June 2015. The A380 also operates on four daily domestic flights between Beijing and Guangzhou.

In January 2012 the second largest South Korean airline, Asiana, announced an order for six A380s for delivery in 2014, the intention being to operate the aircraft on routes to Europe and the USA.

Malaysia Airlines received its first Airbus A380-800 in 2012, having signed a contract for the purchase of six aircraft in 2003. The airline expected to receive its first Airbus A380 in 2007 but delivery was

delayed due to manufacturing problems and the first aircraft was not delivered until May 2012. Six A380s were also ordered by Thai Airways, the first, named *Si Rattana* (a district in northeastern Thailand) being delivered in 2012; the aircraft are configured in the so-called Silk (80 seats) and Royal Silk (12 seats) classes, designed to provide the maximum in comfort and standard of service, in addition to the economy class (485 seats).

The first A380 for All Nippon Airways (ANA) rolled out of the Airbus paintshop in Hamburg, Germany, bearing the airline's distinctive and unique Hawaiian green sea turtle livery. ANA has taken delivery of

Two of Skymark's A380s in long-term storage at Toulouse following the cancellation of the order in 2014. (Airbus)

A British Airways A380 flies in formation with the RAF aerobatic team, the Red Arrows, at the Royal International Air Tattoo, Fairford, Gloucestershire, in July 2013. (British Airways)

three A380s, becoming the first customer for the superjumbo in Japan. The airline took delivery of the first A380 at the end of the first quarter of 2019 and is operating the aircraft on the popular leisure Narita–Honolulu route.

A second Japanese airline, Skymark, placed an order for six A380s in February 2011, but financial troubles experienced by the company led to the order being terminated by Airbus in 2014 after two aircraft had been built.

In 2007, British Airways announced an order for 36 new long-haul aircraft, comprising 12 Airbus A380s and 24 Boeing 787 Dreamliners. Rolls-Royce Trent engines were selected to power both types, with Trent 900s powering the A380s and Trent 1000s powering the 787s. The intention was that the A380s would replace 20 of the airline's Boeing 747-400s. BA's first A380 was delivered on 4 July 2013 and began regular services to Los Angeles on 24 September, followed by Hong Kong on 22 October 2013. In the summer of 2018 Malta-based charter company Hi Fly

became the first in the world to operate second-hand A380s, taking delivery of one aircraft., registered 9H-MIP. This arrived in July 2018 and was sub-leased to Thomas Cook Airlines Scandinavia.

Cancellations

Six A380s were ordered by Virgin Atlantic in 2001. The aircraft were due to be delivered in 2006, but the order was cancelled; Virgin selected the Airbus A350-1000 as its flagship.

In 2012 the A380 appeared set to break into the Russian market when the airline Transaero placed an order for four aircraft. However, delays caused by the worsening economic situation in Russia led to the order being cancelled, and the company ceased operations in 2015.

The Indian company Kingfisher Airlines placed an order for five A380s, an ambitious undertaking in view of the airline's ongoing losses and general poor financial state, but this order was cancelled when Kingfisher ceased operations in 2012.

Special livery

Arguably, no airliner in history has appeared with such exotic and innovative livery as that displayed by the A380, especially those in service with the non-European airlines. In 2019, for example, Emirates produced special liveries to coincide with the ICC Cricket World Cup and also for Arsenal FC. Over the past few years the airline has either applied paintwork or stickers to its aircraft relating to sport, in support of wildlife or in celebration of historical events. In the sporting context, football clubs displaying a special livery on the airline's A380s have included AC Milan, Arsenal and PSG Paris Saint-Germain. In addition to the ICC, Emirates is the main sponsor of events like the FA Cup, the FIFA World Cup and the Rugby World Cup.

Emirates had earlier declared a mission to raise awareness about the threat that illegal wildlife hunting and trade poses to the survival of some of the planet's most endangered and iconic animals. For this reason, the airline supports United for Wildlife, an alliance between seven of the world's most influential wildlife conservation organizations and the British Royal Family. As part of this, the airline has painted two of its A380s in different United for Wildlife liveries. One special livery consists of illustrations of some of the planet's wildlife threatened by poaching and the illegal wildlife trade. The other special livery features drawings of rhinos on the savanna.

In 2018, the United Arab Emirates celebrated the 100th anniversary of the birth of the founding father of the UAE, Sheikh Zayed bin Sultan Al Nayhan. There were multiple celebrations around the country with the largest airlines, Emirates Airlines and Etihad Airways, contributing to the celebrations with several special liveries. Emirates elected to place special stickers on some of its Airbus A380-800s and Boeing 777-300ERs.

Dubai would have hosted the World Expo in 2020 prior to it being postponed as a result of the coronavirus pandemic. Emirates originally placed a World Expo sticker next to the front doors of the aircraft when the agreement to hold the World Expo in Dubai in 2020 was made. In November 2017, the airline painted its first aircraft in special World Expo livery. During the past couple of years the airline has painted several aircraft into three different World Expo liveries. The World Expo livery is based on the Expo 2020 logo, inspired by an ancient gold ring excavated in Dubai. The three different liveries have their own colour and meaning. The colour blue stands

Emirates Airbus A380 A6-EEI, displaying its special wildlife livery, intended to raise awareness of the threat posed to endangered species by hunting and illegal poaching. (Emirates)

Above: 2019 was declared the Year of Tolerance in the UAE. This Emirates A380 displays members of the various ethnic groups resident in the UAE. (Emirates)

Right: An Emirates A380 employs its reverse thrust on a wet runway. Note the Expo 2020 legend on the forward fuselage. (Simon Lowe)

The attractive paintwork displayed on ANA's Airbus A380s depicting the sea turtles that are native to Hawaii. (ANA)

for mobility, orange stands for opportunity and green stands for sustainability. The special liveries are painted on both aircraft types in the Emirates fleet: the Airbus A380-800 and the Boeing 777-300ER. By the end of the World Expo, Emirates would have painted 40 aircraft in the special liveries.

The three ANA A380s are painted in a special livery depicting sea turtles native to Hawaii. The first aircraft is blue, the second green and the third orange. The ANA A380 livery is one of the most elaborate ever painted by Airbus. It took 21 days for the Airbus team to paint a surface of 3,600m² using 16 different shades of colour.

A different view of the original paintwork displayed on ANA's Airbus A380s depicting the sea turtles that are native to Hawaii. (ANA)

Left: Hi Fly, Malta's A380 bearing the special livery designed to draw attention to the fate of the world's coral reefs.
(Hi Fly/Keith Pisani)

Below: In 2019 Qantas decked out its Airbus A380s and Boeing 747s in special paintwork to support the Australian Rugby Union team, the Wallabies, in the Rugby World Cup. The flying kangaroo logo on this A380's tail fin has acquired a gold rugby shirt and green collar. (Qantas)

The A380 Saga

A Summary

The Airbus A380 story is one of a magnificent aircraft that introduced a new standard of luxury and comfort to the world of commercial aviation, but it was a concept dogged from the start by escalating costs and changing political events across the world. Although it would never catch up with the Boeing 747, the feat of engineering that produced it remains almost the stuff of legend. The investment was massive, the programme costing €9.5 billion ($10.7 billion). The prototype obtained its European Union Aviation Safety Agency and Federal Aviation Administration type certificates on 12 December 2006, but then the whole programme was hit by a series of problems.

Difficulties with the electrical wiring caused a two-year delay and saw the development cost rise to €18 billion. It was now clear that the funds allocated to research and development would never be recouped. Later, engine problems were also experienced. The A380 was offered with two powerplant options, the Engine Alliance GP7000 and the Rolls-Royce Trent 900. It was in the latter engine that problems arose with oil leaks causing many engines to be changed at huge cost. During this work cracks were discovered in wing structural fittings which also resulted in mandatory inspections of all A380s and subsequent design changes.

Despite the problems and delays, airline confidence in the A380 remained high. By mid-2019, 15 airlines were operating 238 aircraft throughout the world, the original customer being Singapore Airlines, which launched its first A380 service in October 2007. But further troubles lay ahead. The unit cost of each aircraft rose to $445 million, but even this was insufficient to cover the production costs. Then there was the cost of the infrastructure necessary to bring the components of the A380 together.

Production of the A380 peaked at 30 aircraft per year in 2012 and 2014. Then, in February 2019, the biggest customer, Emirates, announced that it was to reduce its latest order by 39 aircraft in favour of two other Airbus models: the A350 and A330neo, a version using the same engines as the Boeing 787 Dreamliner. For Airbus, it was the last act. The company announced that production of the A380 would cease by 2021.

The end of A380 production has lifted a huge financial burden from the shoulders of Airbus, enabling the consortium to concentrate on the development and production of the later A350. However, the A380 experience will still be available for many years to come. If there is one lesson to be learned from the A380 story, it is perhaps this: reach for the sky, but keep your feet on the ground.

Some airlines decided to reduce their A380 order in favour of a later design, the A350, built in response to the Boeing 787 Dreamliner. The A350-1000 model can seat up to 369 passengers. (Airbus)

Above: Boeing's answer to the requirement for the next generation of long-range airliners is a stretched version of its well-tried 777, the 777-9X, which seats 426 passengers. The airliner features new engines and new technologies. (Boeing)

Right: The crew, inside the cockpit of a Lufthansa Airbus A380, photographed on the ground at Frankfurt. (Steve Jurvetson)

Airbus A380-800 specification

Cockpit crew: 2
Passenger accommodation: 575 typical, 853 maximum
Wingspan: 261ft 8in (79.75m)
Length: 238ft 7in (72.72m)
Height: 79ft (24.09m)
Max takeoff weight: 1,268,000lb (575t)
Empty weight: 611,000lb (277t)
Max payload: 185,000lb (84t)
Fuel capacity: 559,937lb/253,983kg 85,472 US gal/323,546l
Engines: 4 x Rolls-Royce Trent 900 or 4 x GP7200
Max speed: Mach 0.89/586.8mph/ 945km/h
Cruising speed: Mach 0.85/ 560mph/903km/h
Landing speed: 159mph (256km/h)
Service ceiling: 43,000ft (13,100m)
Range: 9,190 miles (14,800km)
Takeoff run at max takeoff weight at sea level: 9,800ft (3,000m)

Airbus A380 economy class. (Bill Holle)

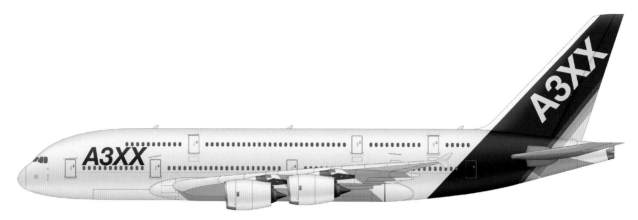

From its very beginning, the Airbus A3XX, as the design was originally known, faced a series of unexpected problems that affected sales projections. The worst of these was a financial crisis that enveloped East Asia in 1997. Airbus had announced its intention to develop its own super-heavy airliner in 1994. Several designs were considered, including an unusual side-by-side combination of two fuselages from its A340. In July 1995, the joint study with Boeing was abandoned, as Boeing's interest in a joint project had declined due to analysis that such a product was unlikely to cover the projected $15 billion development cost. Boeing went on to study a concept known as the New Large Airplane (NLA), an all-new, four-engine 500-seat plus successor to the 747; this too was abandoned in favour of stretched versions of its well-proven 747 series.

The A380 prototype, F-WWOW. The A380 designation was a break from previous Airbus families, which had progressed sequentially from A300 to A340. It was chosen because the number 8 resembles the double-deck cross-section, and is a lucky number in some Asian countries where the aircraft was being marketed. The A380 was the first commercial airliner to have a central wing box made of carbon fibre-reinforced plastic. It is also the first to have a smoothly contoured wing cross–section. This is a variation from the wings of other airliners, which are partitioned into sections along the span. The A380's flowing continuous cross-section reduces aerodynamic drag. Thermoplastics (polymers which have a simple molecular structure comprising chemically independent macromolecules which are softened or melted on heating, then shaped, formed, welded and solidified when cooled) are used in the leading edges of the slats.

The planned A380F in FedEx livery, one of the companies that showed an interest in purchasing the cargo version of the Airbus. The A380F freighter would have been able to lift 150 tonnes of cargo over a range of 5,600nm (10,400km), but although a few initial orders were placed and a combi version envisaged that would be able to carry both freight and passengers, this model was cancelled so that Airbus could give priority to production of the A380-800 passenger version.

The launch customer for the A380 was Singapore Airlines, which announced an order for up to 25 Airbus A3XXs (as the A380 was known at the time) on 29 September 2000. The deal, costing $8.6 billion, involved a firm order for ten aircraft with options on 15 more airframes. After some delay caused by technical problems, Singapore Airlines took delivery of its first A380 (9V-SKA) on 15 October 2007. Route flying with this aircraft began on 25 October 2007 with flight number SQ380 operating between Singapore and Sydney. SIA began regular services with the A380 on 28 October 2007. Two months later, Singapore Airlines' CEO Chew Choong Seng stated the A380 was performing better than either the airline or Airbus had anticipated, burning 20 percent less fuel per seat mile than the airline's 747-400 fleet.

Two of Singapore Airlines' A380s were painted in special livery to celebrate Singapore's Golden Jubilee. The special livery featured a 10m-tall and 47m-long Singapore flag-themed design on both sides of the fuselage. The livery was retained until the end of 2015. This livery is featured on die-cast models of the airliner which are available for purchase by model enthusiasts.

An Airbus A380 in the livery of Emirates which became by far the biggest customer for the airline. The original deal involved five A380-800 passenger aircraft and two freighter versions. The deal was confirmed on 4 November 2001 when Emirates announced orders for 15 more A380-800s. An additional order for 21 A380-800s was placed two years later. In April 2006 Emirates replaced its order for the two freighter variants with an order for two A380-800s. The eventual Emirates A380 order rose to 142 aircraft, the 100th aircraft joining the fleet on October 2017. Then, in February 2019, following a review of its operations, Emirates cancelled most of the A380s it still had on order, cutting the number still to be delivered to just fourteen.

The second Middle Eastern airline to place an order for the A380 was Etihad Airways, the flag carrier airline of the United Arab Emirates, which began operations in November 2003. Etihad announced an order for four A380s on 20 July 2004, which was increased to ten in July 2008, with options on a further five. The aircraft were all to be powered by the Engine Alliance GP7200. The first commercial flight by an Etihad A380 took place on 27 December 2014, when A6-APA flew from Abu Dhabi to London Heathrow. Etihad Airways had its A380s painted in various schemes, including one in 2018 commemorating the 100th anniversary of the birth of Sheikh Zayed bin Sultan al Nahyan, founding father of the UAE.

Qatar Airways was the third Middle Eastern airline to order the A380, making its first commercial flight with the type from Doha to London on 10 October 2014. The distinctive Qatar Airways logo, seen here on the tail, depicts the head of an oryx, an antelope with very long straight horns, which is the nation's national animal.

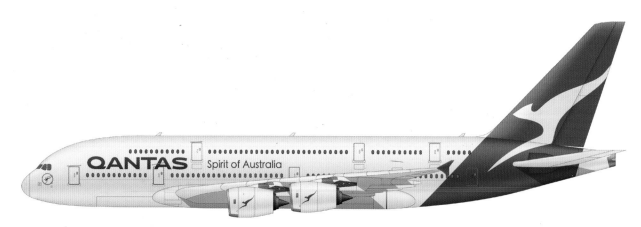

Qantas, the Australian national carrier, placed an order for 12 A380-800s, beginning passenger services between Melbourne and Los Angeles in October 2008. By the end of the year their A380s had carried 890,000 passengers on 2,200 flights over five major routes, totalling 21,000 flying hours. It was this example, VH-OQA, that suffered serious damage as a result of an uncontained engine failure and explosion in November 2010. The aircraft was repaired and returned to service in April 2012.

Airbus A380 F-HPJA in the colours of Air France, the first European airline to operate the type. The aircraft illustrated, F-HPJE, was the second to experience an uncontained engine failure in an incident that occurred over Greenland on 20 September 2017. The aircraft was repaired and returned to service in January 2018, but was later placed in storage.

Hard on Air France's heels as an A380 customer was the German airline Lufthansa, which on 6 December 2001 announced an order for 15 aircraft with ten more options. The aircraft were to be used exclusively for long-haul flights from Frankfurt. This example, D-AIMB, bore the name *München*. It was the 38th A380 to fly.

China Southern Airlines became the only Chinese airline to order the A380, acquiring five aircraft which were initially operated on the Beijing–Guangzhou and Beijing–Hong Kong routes. The airline's distinctive bright red logo, superimposed on the blue tail fin, represents the kapok flower, which proliferates in the airline's home city of Guangzhou, the capital of Guangdou province in southern China.

Korean Air introduced the first of ten A380s into service on 17 June 2011. Korean Air's international passenger division, and related subsidiary cargo division, together serve 126 cities in 44 countries. Its domestic division serves 13 destinations. It is among the top 20 airlines in the world in terms of passengers carried and is also one of the top-ranked international cargo airlines.

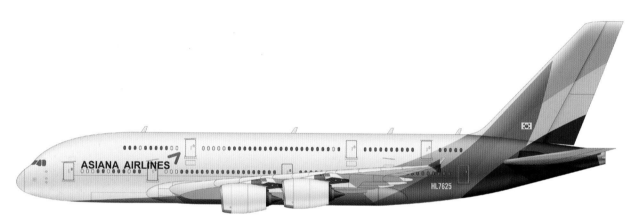

In January 2012 the second-largest South Korean airline, Asiana, announced an order for six A380s for delivery in 2014. The intention was to operate the aircraft on routes to Europe and the USA. The aircraft seen here, HL7625, made the airline's first commercial A380 flight from Seoul to Tokyo on 13 June 2014.

Malaysia Airlines received its first Airbus A380-800 in June 2012, having signed a contract for the purchase of six aircraft in 2003. The Airline's first commercial A380 flight was made by this aircraft, 9M-MNA, from Kuala Lumpur to London Heathrow on 1 July 2012.

Six A380s were ordered by Thai Airways, the first, named *Si Rattana* (a district in northeastern Thailand) being delivered in 2012. The aircraft are configured in the so-called Silk (80 seats) and Royal Silk (12 seats) classes, designed to provide the maximum comfort and standard of service, in addition to the economy class (485 seats).

The first A380 for All Nippon Airways (ANA) rolled out of the Airbus paintshop in Hamburg, Germany, bearing the airline's distinctive and unique Hawaiian green sea turtle livery. Three ANA A380s are painted in the special livery depicting sea turtles, which are native to Hawaii. The first aircraft, pictured here, is blue, the second green and the third orange. The ANA A380 livery is one of the most elaborate ever painted by Airbus. It took 21 days for the Airbus team to paint a surface of 3,600m² using 16 different shades of colour.

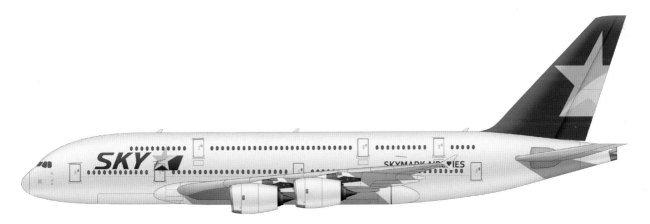

A second Japanese airline, Skymark, placed an order for six A380s in February 2011, but financial troubles experienced by the company led to the order being terminated by Airbus in 2014 after two aircraft had been built. The first of these, JA380A, was converted to A380-842 configuration and was delivered to Emirates in November 2018. In the following year, registered A6-EVB, it was painted in the special Year of Tolerance livery shown here.

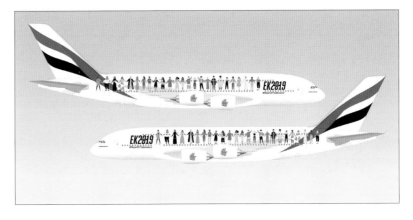

The A380 in the distinctive livery of British Airways. In 2007, British Airways announced an order for 36 new long-haul aircraft, comprising 12 Airbus A380s and 24 Boeing 787 Dreamliners. Rolls-Royce Trent engines were selected to power both types, with Trent 900s powering the A380s and Trent 1000s powering the 787s. The intention was that the A380s would replace 20 of the airline's Boeing 747-400s. BA's first A380 was delivered on 4 July 2013 and began regular services to Los Angeles on 24 September, followed by Hong Kong on 22 October 2013.

In the summer of 2018, Malta-based charter company Hi Fly became the first in the world to operate second-hand A380s, taking delivery of one aircraft, registered 9H-MIP. This arrived in July 2018 and was sub-leased to Thomas Cook Airlines Scandinavia. On its return to Hi Fly it was subsequently wet-leased to Air Austral, Air Senegal, Aerolineas Estelar Latinoamerica and Norwegian Air Shuttle before once again returning to Hi Fly. In 2020, leased to the Mirpuri Foundation, it was painted in a coral-themed livery to advertise the foundation's campaign to save the world's coral reefs.

This is how a Virgin Atlantic A380 would have appeared if the airline had not cancelled its order in favour of the Airbus A350-1000.

The Russian airline Aeroflot had plans to operate the A380 aircraft ordered by another Russian airline, Transaero, but the order was cancelled after the latter company ceased operations in 2015.

The Indian company Kingfisher Airlines placed an order for five A380s, an ambitious undertaking in view of the airline's ongoing losses and general poor financial state. This order was cancelled when Kingfisher ceased operations in 2012.

The A380 as it would have appeared in the colours of the defunct Russian airline Transaero.

Modelling the A380

Airbus A380-800
Revell 1/144
Modelled by Glenn Ashley

The 1/144 Revell kit is the most accessible option for modellers wishing to build an A380. This kit has been issued in several boxings with markings for various airlines. My initial boxing was a British Airways one but shortly after construction disaster struck at the painting stage. When the white was applied from an aerosol can it reacted with the plastic and everything simply bubbled up. That kit was scrapped and a second version was purchased. This time I went for the Emirates version that

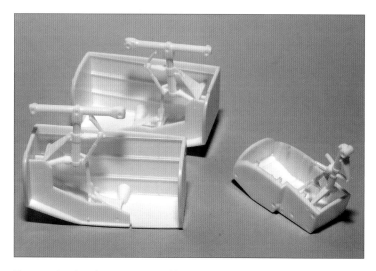

The original boxing of the Revell 1/144-scale A380 I intended to build, with its British Airways decals. This was replaced with boxing featuring an Emirates aircraft.

The completed undercarriage assemblies, minus wheels, at an early stage of the construction. As can be seen these are quite complicated and fragile, being moulded to scale.

features wildlife artwork along both sides of the fuselage.

Construction started with the cavernous fuselage. First I assembled the cockpit interior but soon decided I would paint over the windows and use the decals to represent these. I noticed, that with the relatively thin plastic used, there could possibly be issues with the fuselage flexing during construction due simply to the size of the fuselage and the total lack of any bulkheads included to help keep the full assembly rigid. Before the two halves were put together I had to assemble the nose-wheel bay. I opted to add the main undercarriage bays until I had sorted the fuselage out. In order to get as strong a fuselage joint as possible, I used tube cement and held the fuselage halves together using tape. This was left aside to dry for a couple of days.

With the fuselage drying I turned to assembling the main undercarriage bays and gear. This is one part of the kit where you could really do with an extra set of hands, or two. The legs are moulded to scale, making them quite fragile so take your time when assembling these. I took time assembling the basic legs as each comprises four separate pieces, and are obviously quite small and fiddly. I used Tamiya Extra Thin quick-setting cement for all assemblies such as this. Fitting the assembled legs into their respective bays is a feat that will test your patience, unless you have three hands and work in keyhole surgery. Yes, it is small and complex, and trying to line everything up will have you pushed to the limits at times. Even once it is all assembled the main gear assembly still has a very fragile feel to it. So be warned, it is very easily broken. I left these assemblies out until I had sanded down the fuselage joints. When I added them, I used Revell Contacta cement to get a good strong construction. I left the wheels themselves off at this stage with the plan to add them later in the build.

This was all left aside to set completely. Next I turned to assembling the main wings. These are a simple two-part assembly done with Contacta and the halves were held together with strips of Tamiya masking tape.

Once the wings were offered up to the fuselage it was found they weren't a great fit. They needed a little trimming in order to get a reasonable fit. This could be due to mould wear. After all, the kit has been out for a few years now and in various boxings. Be careful not to try and force the fit of the wings or you may pop the upper fuselage joint. This is where some decent bulkheads would have been a big bonus. Something kit manufacturers might consider with kits that feature large cavernous empty fuselages.

With the wings and fuselage together I added nose weight in the front of the aircraft by adding three large nuts, from B&Q, as weight. These were dipped in Araldite epoxy glue before being slid into the front fuselage via the underside opening. They were left to set completely before anything else was done on the main part of the model. Once these had set, the lower fuselage piece was to be added (part 149). As this too was potentially a very weak joint I added two pieces of thick plasticard at the front and rear of the opening to give the part something to attach to. The part itself needs slight trimming to get a good fit, again secured with Contacta cement. The two forward undercarriage doors can be added at the same time.

The next items for assembly were the flap actuators which needed some cleaning up of the joints once assembled. These had gaps once fitted to the fuselage which were filled with white glue, with the excess wiped off using a damp cotton bud. Also at this stage I assembled the tailplanes.

With all joint lines cleaned up I gave the entire model a coat of Halfords Grey Primer to check for any areas that would need further work. A few little areas showed up but overall the construction was looking good. The plan was to leave the engines off until later in the build to avoid any chance

The nose wheel assembly has to be fitted before the fuselage halves can be assembled. This makes it a possible breakage item during assembly so take care with it.

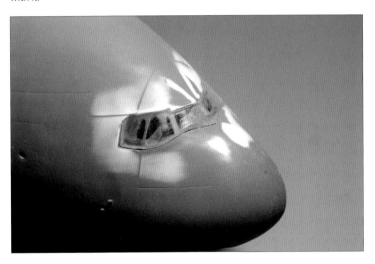

A view of the kit windscreen, which is not the best-fitting part of the kit. Here it is in the process of being sanded down to improve the fit. I opted to paint over it and use the decals instead. The edges would be filled with superglue, then the area sanded down for a smooth finish prior to painting.

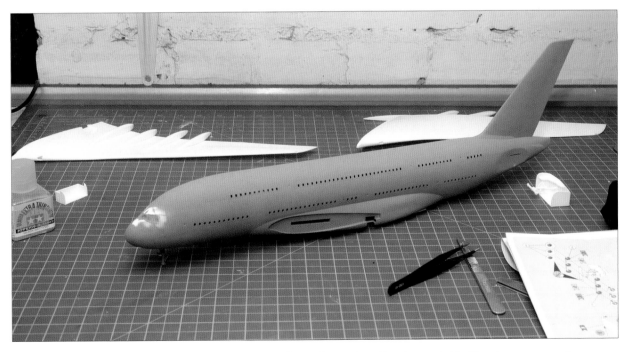

The assembled fuselage joints sanded down and given an overall coat of grey primer. The wings are behind it, and as you can see, it dominates any modelling bench by its sheer size.

of damage. So the model was basically ready for painting.

I sanded the entire model down using 1200 grit wet or dry to get as smooth a finish as possible. Then the model was wiped down using B&Q decorator's wipes to remove any remaining dirt.

I opted to paint the fuselage first using Halfords Gloss White straight from the aerosol can. This was misted on in three

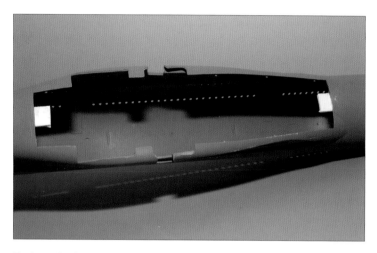

The lower fuselage section was test-fitted and there was clearly a little warping of the kit part here. This could possibly result in a very weak joint due to the thinness of the plastic.

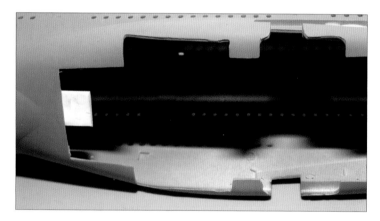

In order to avoid this weak joint two pieces of 20-thou plasticard were glued into the front and rear of the opening to act as a key to cement the lower fuselage section on to.

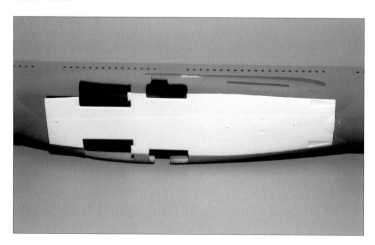

A closer view of the rear tab of plasticard. The extent of flash on the moulding of the kit can also be seen. The moulds clearly show some degree of wear on their edges.

light coats to get a good balanced finish without any runs. Take your time with this stage and don't try to rush it. As is the norm with gloss paint the model was put aside for a couple of days to cure fully. The model had a nice smooth finish that was going to be ready for the mass of decals that would later be added.

Once the fuselage was dry, I masked off the wings and tailplanes for painting. You will certainly make use of plenty of masking tape when building this model. The wings and tailplanes were then sprayed light grey. I used RAF Barley Grey as it seemed a fairly good match. Being acrylic paint, it dried fairly quickly and then the fun started. The upper wings have sections that are a darker grey colour and this is where your masking off skills will be tested. The grey panels don't match up fully to panel lines and some of it is down to careful alignment of tape. The inner rear portion is curved to make things even worse, and to top it off there are black cheat lines to be added after.

For the curved section I simply copied the decal sheet using my flatbed scanner to copy that portion of the decal sheet to make a mask to fit. These inner sections were sprayed neutral grey which also seemed a good match. Once dry the wings were given a coat of gloss varnish prior to the start of decaling.

First of all I opted to add the black lines to the wings and see how well things lined up. I have to say most of them lined up ideally but there were a couple of areas that would need masking and a little correcting with the airbrush. Once the decals had dried overnight, the wings were given another coat of gloss varnish to seal the decals in before masking off any areas that needed a bit of correcting. There is no quick and easy way round all of this. Patience is the key here.

Once the wings were done, it was time to turn to the very attractive fuselage decals. First of all I added the tail stripes. These settled down superbly and were a joy to add. These should be left to dry before moving onto the next stage. This boxing features a stunning gallery of animals along both fuselage sides. They are split into smaller sections. Here again, work in small stages and ensure the decals all line up correctly. You will find some of the animal decals need to be laid over others, although the instructions don't mention this. They are designed by Daco Productions in Belgium who have an excellent reputation for their products. The decals were dipped in warm water for a few seconds then placed on kitchen roll to allow the decal to separate from the backing paper. Only work on one decal at a time or you will have problems. I used Mr Mark Setter and Micro Sol decal solutions to give me a wet surface on which to slide the decal. Once correctly positioned, I removed any excess fluid using a cotton bud and left each decal to dry out before adding the next one. I added all the animal

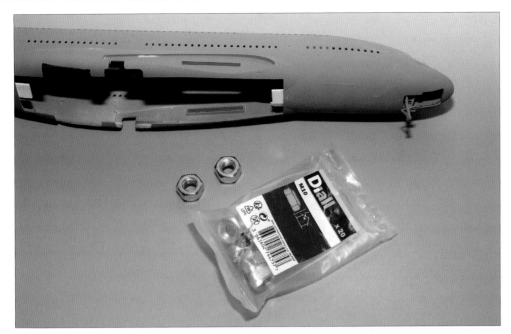

The next step is to add nose weight in the kit so it is not a tail sitter. This was done using large metal nuts secured using two-part epoxy cement. These should be allowed to set fully before any further work can be carried out.

Next to fit were the main undercarriage units into either side of the central fuselage.

decals first and allowed these to dry out as further decals would be laid over them. Once the decals are added, do not touch them. With decal solutions you may see the decal wrinkle slightly but leave it, as this is part of the natural process. You could end up spoiling your model otherwise.

Next was the task of adding the window and door decals. These were added in sections allowing those to dry out before adding the next batch. After this it was simply a case of carefully working through all the smaller decals, stencils and other fuselage markings.

With all of this laid aside to dry out, I now turned to start work on the engines. These need to be built in stages too. Starting with the engine inners which, once assembled, were given a coat of silver paint. The inner parts of the engine nacelles were painted grey before the engines were built. I left

the engine front sections off until the main portions of the engines were painted. The engines were given a coat of white before the engine fronts were added. These were then decaled up as well.

The next step was to add a little weathering to the model. An internet search showed that some A380s look gleaming and brand new while others are certainly showing wear and tear on their finishes. On the wings I added a wash of Payne's grey oil paint thinned heavily with white spirit. This was then applied over the panel lines with a thin brush and left to dry for around 30 minutes. Once dry, the excess was rubbed off using kitchen roll and, finally, with an old handkerchief. This left some residue in the panel lines as well as a little streaking across the wings. Always work with the airflow direction on a model when doing this. You will find the wash collects in the right places and any streaking goes in the direction of air flowing over the wing surfaces. As clean as an airliner may look, it is still a working machine and picks up a degree of dirt along the way. On the undersides of the fuselage I carefully added some weathering using the airbrush to add some dirt with Alclad Transparent Smoke, working at low pressure and not overdoing it. This was applied using an airbrush at a low pressure setting and adjusting the nozzle to a very fine spray pattern before building this up gradually.

Once this was complete, I added the engines to the wings before adding the wheels, and there are enough of them. All that still needed to be added were a few small aerials, undercarriage doors and to give the model an overall coat of satin varnish in order to give it a common finish. In this case I mixed gloss and matt varnish 50/50 then thinned it down 70 percent with thinners and 30 percent varnish before spraying it all over the model.

I have to say there were aspects of the model that were a challenge and somewhat frustrating in some respects, but that is not to say it is not a good kit, just one that needs a fair degree of care, especially with the smaller, more fragile assemblies.

Once the main undercarriage units are fitted, they should be allowed to set completely. They were added using Revell Contacta cement for a more secure fit.

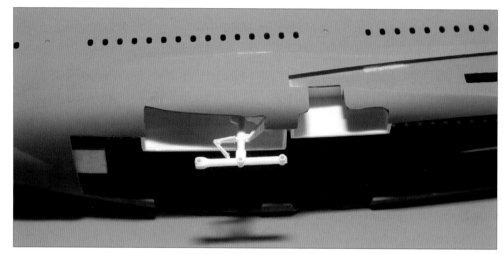

Once all had set, the lower fuselage panel was fitted and held in place using strips of Tamiya masking tape. This was due to the slight warping of this part.

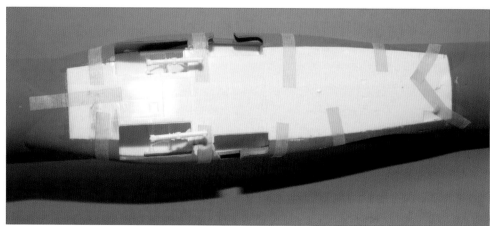

The wings, ready to have the flap actuator fairings fitted. These were assembled and the relevant joint lines were cleaned up before they were fitted.

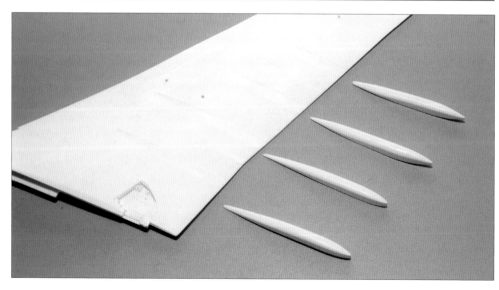

Aftermarket products

There are not many aftermarket items available due to the nature and scale of the Revell kit but those found are listed below.

CANOPY MASKS
KV Models:
KV14646 – Window and wheel paint masks for the Revell kit

ETCHED BRASS DETAIL SETS
Metallic Details:
MDMD14418 – Exterior Detail Set. This includes areas such as the engines, aircraft undersides and pitot tubes etc.

DECALS
26 Decals:
STS44154 – Korean Air markings
STS44217 – Qatar Airways markings
SYS44218 – Thai Airways markings

Draw Decals:
A380-2 – TNT Cargo markings
A380-3 – Pan-Am markings
A380-4 – Baniff International markings
A380-5 – Baniff markings

A380-6 – Airwest markings
A380-7 – Lufthansa markings
A380-9 – Lufthansa markings

Giodecals:
144-492 – ANA Airways 'Blue' markings
144-497 – Etihad Airways markings
144-510 – ANA Airways 'Orange' markings
144-517 – Emirates 'Wildlife 2' markings
144-564 – ANA Airways 'Green' markings

TB Decals:
TBD76 – Qantas markings
TBD77 – British Airways markings
TBD78 – Air France markings
TBD153 – Thai Airways markings
TBD191 – Emirates Airlines markings
TBD192 – Singapore Airlines markings
TBD193 – Air Korean markings
TBD211 – Qatar Airways markings
TBD214 – Malaysia Airways markings
TBD225 – China Southern markings
TBD308 – Lufthansa new tail logo markings
TBD353 – Airbus 50th Anniversary Logo Prototype markings
TBD392 – ANA Airlines KAI markings
TBD393 – ANA Airlines Ka La markings
TBD391 – ANA Airlines LANI JA markings

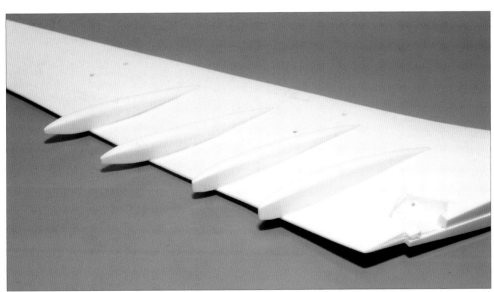

Once fitted, there were a few small gaps between the wings and the fairings. These were filled with white glue with the excess removed using a damp cotton bud.

The fuselage was painted using Halfords Gloss White applied in three light coats. Don't try to paint the entire fuselage in one quick go, or you may get paint runs. The wings had also been painted by now with a few little areas to be touched up. A couple of small gaps appeared around the windscreen but were refilled before the decals were added to replace them.

After spraying the wings with RAF Barley Grey for the lighter shade, the inner sections were masked off and sprayed with Neutral Grey.

The opposite wing after the masking had been removed. The kit had no real guidelines for masking as the darker areas did not always match to panel lines. A little touching up would be required.

After a coat of gloss varnish on the wings, it was time to start adding the decals. Using one of the various decal application fluids makes things a lot easier. Two options are Mr Mark or Micro Set/Sol.

With the bulk of the decals added, they were sealed with a coat of gloss varnish to protect them. This would be required on the wings when the panel line wash was added.

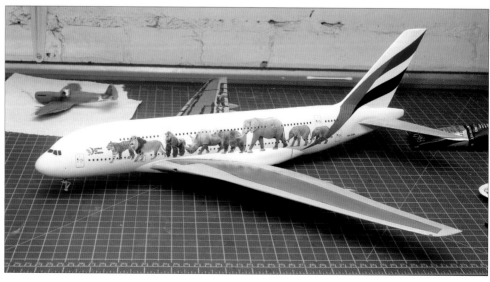

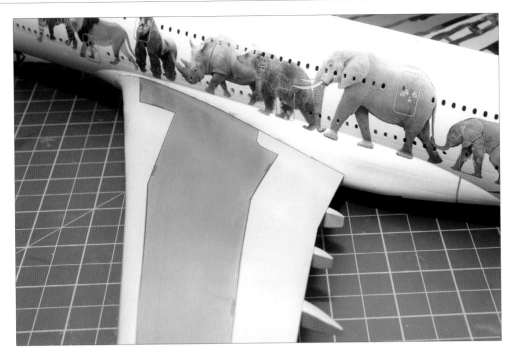

The wing walkway lines matched up fairly well to the masking with only a couple of places that needed filling in.

The wing panel lines were given a wash of thinned-down grey oil paint applied with a fine brush. The paint was thinned with white spirit to the consistency of milk.

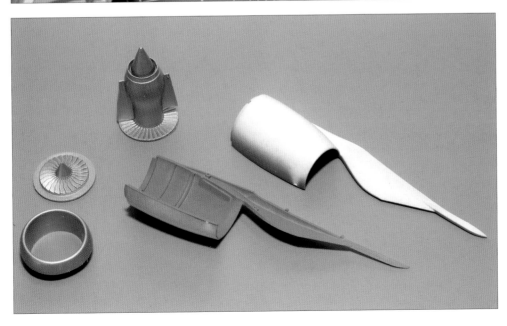

The engines were part-painted before assembly, the inner engine parts in silver and the inside of the nacelles in grey.

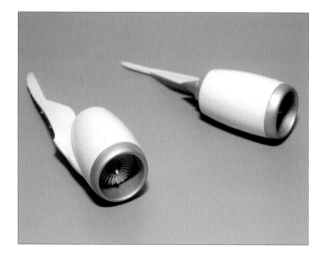

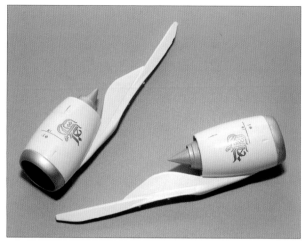

The assembled nacelles after being painted white and having the silver engine fronts fitted.

The completed engine units after decals were added. There are quite a few decals to add to this aircraft. It is quite surprising for an airliner in this scale.

A view of the upper starboard wing showing how the panel wash highlights the detail and gives an in-service look to the aircraft.

A view of the nose of the model showing the windscreen decals which covered the poorly fitting, clear kit parts. Even in this scale they feature windscreen wipers.

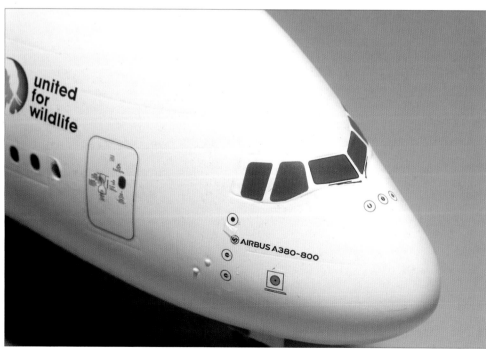

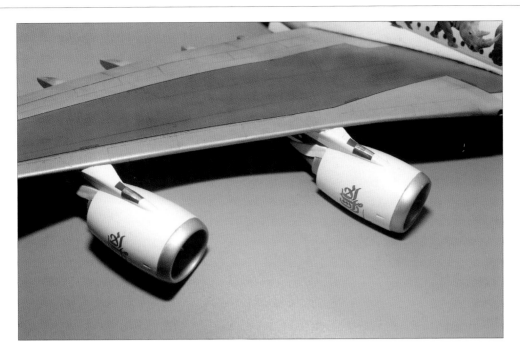

When all four engines were completed, they were fitted under each wing. The fit of these was actually very good.

Decaling completed, and as well as the very colourful animal artwork, the kit features decals for all the windows which gives a much better effect to the completed model.

A view of the underside of the model showing dirt using transparent smoke paint applied carefully using an airbrush. This gives an impression of the dirt that can build up on the underside of an aircraft during operations.

Airbus A380-800
Revell 1/144
Modelled by Ben Skipper

First released in 2002 and then in 2018 with BA's distinctive livery, Revell's 163-part kit for this giant of the skies, the Airbus A380-800, really is a testament to the company's policy of providing the modeller with the most eclectic kits in town. Before going any further it is worth pointing out that this kit truly isn't for the beginner, but if you're up for the challenge then do have a go.

The large lid-opening box contains seven sprues and a huge decal sheet. Modellers are treated to Revell's new-look colour instructions which are a triumph of graphic design. Clear, with wonderful illustrations and easy-to-follow steps with only a few moments of confusion, which in fairness were probably of my own making. They really make the kit assembly a joy to plan.

The kit's engraved details are well planned but, for scale, may be a little too deep. However, they make the model stand out and for the super detailers out there they are a weathering paradise. Revell have clearly researched the prototype well, so my only request would be that the wing root light apertures that were present on Airbus's own prototypes remain for the in-service kit examples. However, nothing a little bit of filler and some judicious sanding won't cure.

Not surprisingly, the A380's size, even in 1/144 scale, demands a very considered and measured approach to construction. The wings were glued together small sections at a time, resting overnight and clamped with metal bulldog clips. The gull wing shape became more prevalent as the wing halves were brought together. Once the glue had cured, the wings were surprisingly strong with no flex whatsoever.

After constructing the simple cockpit and adding a pilot figure from PECO's N Gauge range of platform figures, the fuselage halves were assembled. Again, due to size, this was glued together in stages using natural rubber bands and spreader bars made from sprue. Taking time with this process is the key to a great finish. There was slight warping, which led to some overlapping, but this was easily sanded out.

The engines were quick and simple to put together and give a great representation of the Rolls-Royce Trent 900 units. Along with the flap track fairings, the engine mounts did need some attention with filler where they met the wing's surface.

The last big hurdle was the undercarriage set. Taking time is key to a good result here and planning how the completed set will fit is also important. These are also where previous modelling skills come in handy as they are complex units and it pays to really study the instruction before setting forth with knife and glue.

Left: The first task was to remove the wing assemblies from the sprues. These interesting-looking oblong mounts were best removed with a razor saw.

Below: The stabilizers are pretty straightforward two-piece constructions and go together like a dream.

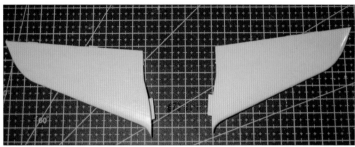

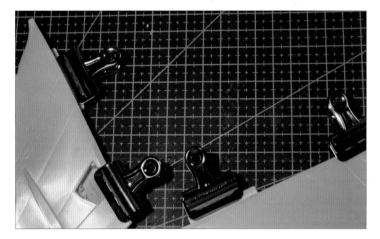

Revell have gone all out to cast the main wing assemblies with their distinctive gull wing form. As a result, the wings have to be cemented in a series of small stages. Start at the roots and work down to the tips using bulldog clips to keep the sections together.

A PECO N Gauge figure has been added to the cockpit to look like a pilot.

The cockpit was primed with Halfords Grey Primer and then painted with a base coat of Tamiya XF83 Medium Sea Grey. The cockpit details are painted using a range of Citadel and Tamiya colours. Online resources are great for detailing ideas, especially seat colours. The cabin door recess received a lining wash of Citadel Chaos Black. The captain is making sure everything is ready for departure.

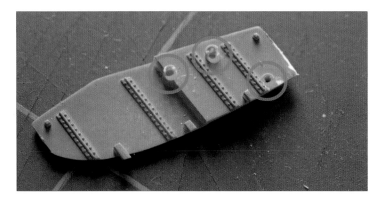

The nose landing gear looks to be fragile so the mounts have been cut into cups so that the gear can be popped in after spraying.

Above: The nose landing gear is beautifully cast by Revell. There is a lot of flash on the moulding here that needs careful removal: a sharp modelling knife blade is a must.

Right: The floor plate of the fuselage is now in place. Note the undercarriage mounts have been cut like the nose undercarriage. A strip of plastic has been inserted to support the undercarriage once in place.

Painting and finishing was easy enough. I found the colour guides supplied by Revell spot on and made life a little easier by saving research time. Here the kit-supplied British Airways finish has been used. BA blue will always be a source of contention, so consider scale colour. Simply put, use slightly lighter shades of paint when painting dark surfaces, and in this instance, Tamiya's Sky Blue really does hit the mark.

The decals are beautifully printed with wonderful colour registration and react well to copious amounts of Micro Sol setting solution. The instructions are best studied first and then broken down into sections. The whole process is a day's work, but the results are stunning and transform the kit into a model.

The overall shape of the kit and its surface details really bear up to scrutiny and should satisfy the most discerning of modelling tastes. Even though the kit is over 15 years old, it's still a great buy and one which teaches as much as it entertains. The added bonus is that you know, with Revell, revised A380 liveries will always be on their way.

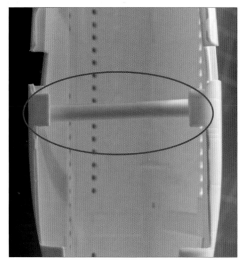

The fuselage comes in three sections. The two main sections are glued together slowly, a piece at a time. The halves are then held together with an elastic band and a piece of sprue is cut to provide a beam that keeps the fuselage halves at roughly the right distance where the bottom plate will be added.

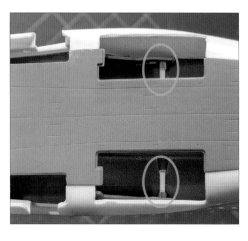

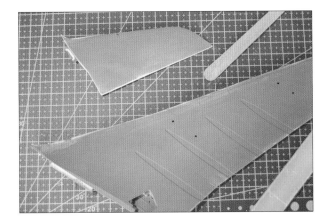

The wings and stabilizers were primed and areas which had been filled were rubbed down.

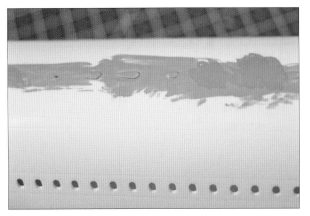

As with all things the fuselage halves needed a bit of attention where the two halves meet. Mr Surfacer 1000 is used to eliminate scratches and joins. In some places a couple of coats were applied. Mr Surfacer is great for addressing those fine join lines that occasionally turn up, easy to apply and easy to sand.

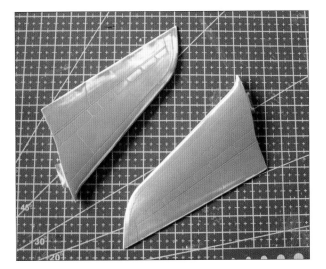

Stabilizers are sanded once more to level the Mr Surfacer joint fillings.

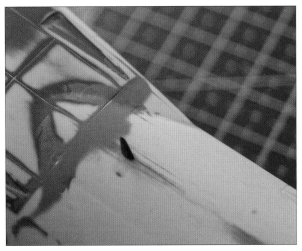

The process of sanding down the Mr Surfacer on the fuselage patches is best achieved with 1000 grit wet or dry, with the emphasis on wet. The first primer coat will, undoubtedly, reveal any areas that need attention. Allow the primer coats to sit for at least 12 hours to harden. If priming in a damp atmosphere, dry the surface with a hairdryer on medium heat to help eliminate trapped moisture.

The fuselage, due to its size, produced some challenges in terms of join steps. The time spent sanding, often quite brutally, and filling, has produced a wonderful result which is as much a testament to the overall quality of the kits as it is to the modeller's resolve.

The engine fans are now painted with a mix of Revell and Citadel acrylics. These are brush painted and the layers of mixed colours are applied as combinations of thinned washes and dry brushing. The end result of this patient approach is a wonderfully iridescent feel to the fan blades with their copper sheen, reminiscent of the prototype Airbus A380.

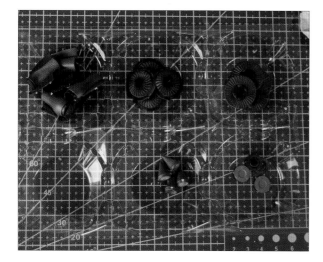

Old-style cupcake holders are great for keeping bits and pieces safe prior to assembly.

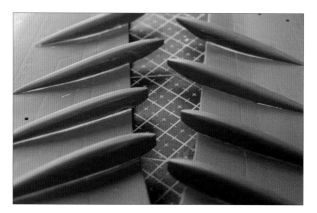

Once you're happy that the gap is filled, smooth the putty with a wet cotton bud. As the putty is water based, it cleans up easily and is great for filling corners like this. Here the gaps are filled and ready for another coat of primer. The putty dries quickly and smoothly.

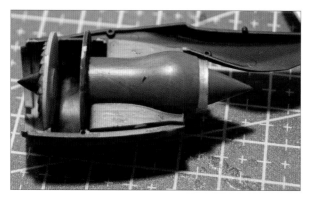

The painting now starts in earnest with the fuselage receiving multiple coats of highly thinned Tamiya X2.

Sadly there are some pretty large gaps in between the flap track fairings and the lower wing surface. Vallejo Plastic Putty is a boon in a situation like this. First step is to squeeze some of the putty into the gap and smooth it with a shaping tool, or a cocktail stick with a wedge shape cut into it.

The next stage is to assemble the engines. While these are simple representations they are nicely replicated and fall together well.

Left: The engines and front fans are placed in one side of the nacelle and glued into place with Tamiya's extra thin glue.

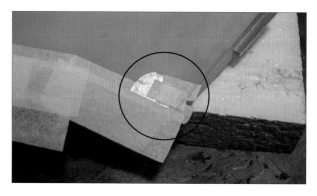

The wings are given several light coats of Tamiya XF-55 Deck Tan, an excellent match for the grey Revell has identified in their instructions. Circled is the small section of Frisket film cut into a curve using a French circle and a steady hand. The rest of the masking is for the darker grey fill.

The white main colour is sprayed on in thin layers at a low air pressure to prevent splatter and air drying. Soon the fuselage is starting to look more than presentable.

The next stage of painting is the blue of the lower fuselage and engine nacelles. This calls for some inventive masking and more than a few post-it notes.

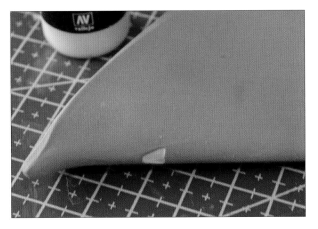

The large light apertures of the kit aren't prototype accurate. The triangular light array has disappeared and has been replaced by a strip of three lights. Out with the filler once more.

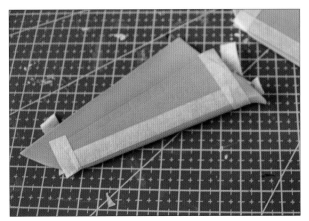

The stabilizers are varnished with a coat of quick-drying Humbrol Gloss Cote in readiness for decal application. Before this final stage the leading edges are painted with Citadel Mithril Silver.

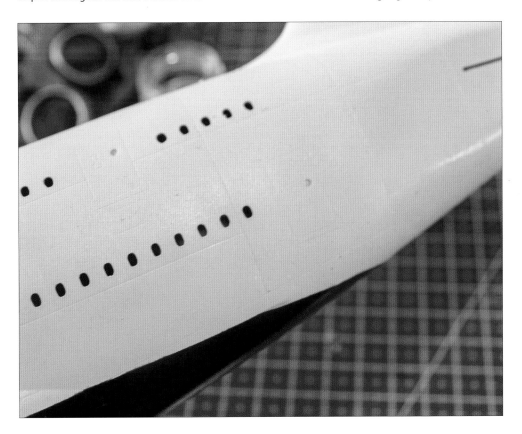

The masking for the blue lower hull is removed. The kink in the blue line will be addressed with some delicate brushwork. The blue is Tamiya X3 and is an excellent match for the almost-indigo shades of British Airways' own blues.

The once-gaping aperture of the wing light is now filled and ready for a fresh cover of paint. The RAF medium sea grey of the wing insert is from Hannats Xtracrylix range of paints.

Now the painting is complete it's time for the decals to be applied. I've started with the long strip that runs down the length of the rudder. It's a bit tricky but is helped into place with some Micro Sol setting fluid.

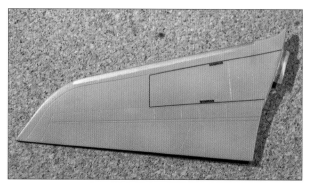

The first of the British Airways branding is applied to the fuselage. The gloss finish is important as it helps hide the carrier film.

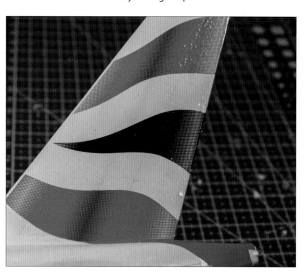

So as not to weaken the plastic of the wheel sets, attach the pieces with superglue. This provides strength for weak points and ensures that joints aren't further weakened by solvent-based glues.

Above: By far the largest decal is the tail decal. A few coats of Micro Sol will transform this decal finish into one that appears to be painted.

Right: Some decals lie over one another at various points so it's important to let one layer dry before applying the next.

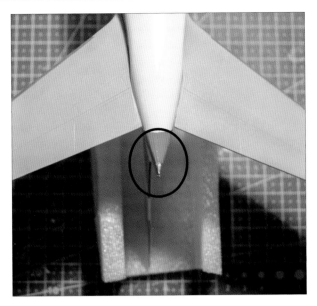

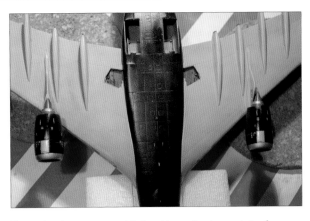

The main wings are now added and lower fuselage points of interest, such as antenna arrays, are finished in gloss white, while the lower flight light is painted, providing a much needed visual break in the sea of blue. Note the red tip finishes to the flap track fairings.

The stabilizers are glued into position and last-minute paint details are applied. Note the APU exhaust pipe shroud finished in Citadel Mithril Silver.

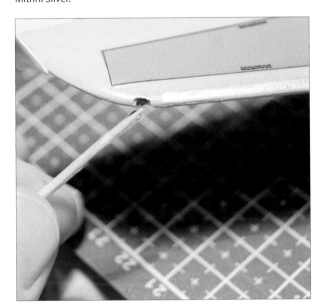

The wing light plastic lenses were a little too fiddly, so Humbrol Clearfix was used to make the light covers. The first task was to paint the correct colours of lights on both wings and then surround the void edges with Clearfix so that subsequent layers had something to stick to. Once dry, the Clearfix was drawn across with a cocktail stick to produce the Perspex effect.

The last bit of assembly, the undercarriage. Taking the time to make the notches earlier helped with easing the assembled wheel sets into place. The final touch will be the doors glued into place.

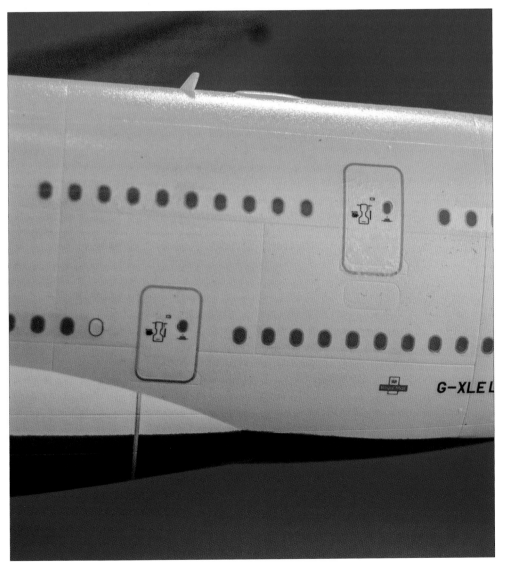

A combination of Tamiya acrylics and Alclad Stainless Lacquer for the APU exhaust and engine cans. The two engines on the right still have masking tape in place after being sprayed steel and black.

Placement of the engine decals can be found on pages 18 and 19 of the kit's instructions. A few photos downloaded from the internet can't hurt either to help with correct positioning.

Airbus A380-800
Heller 1/144
Modelled by Brian Richardson

Heller released its 1/125 kit around 2010 and has since reboxed it with Air France and Lufthansa decals. This kit represents the first prototype, F-WWOW, and has the special livery on the decal sheet for this version. The 43 pages of instructions are well laid out and clearly depict the sequence of the build. Careful study is required when it comes to painting and applying the decals. Page 6 has a list of colours required but curiously doesn't name the brand. After checking the listed paint numbers it turns out they are Humbrol enamels. Those with the prefix M have to be mixed from a combination of different colours. In this build Tamiya acrylics have been used and the colours matched as closely as possible.

This is a big kit with a relatively small parts count and should have been an easy build. Unfortunately, it is plagued by poor fit and sink marks, lots of sink marks. The fuselage is assembled in five sections from the cockpit to the tail. This is where most of the filling and sanding is required. It is moulded in white which is big help when painting. Other parts are coloured grey or silver to match the real components. The passenger and cargo doors are moulded separately but as there's minimal interior provided, they've been closed up. This requires more trimming, filling and sanding to get a good fit. The wings and tail in this kit were warped and some success was achieved with hot water trying to straighten them. However, no amount of clamping and hot water would coerce the left wing into its characteristic gull-wing shaped droop. Heller's decal sheets (there are two) are the kit's saving grace, with good register and accurate colours. The carrier film is super thin and at the same time quite strong, allowing handling and easy placement without having the decal shatter or fold over on itself as some tend to do. Some of the window frames didn't quite line up properly. The easy fix is to cut between every second or third one to correct the misalignment. These also respond well to decal softener which will be required when applying the tail fin flash and door decals.

It's disappointing. Heller could have had an award-winning model in the range but they've dropped the ball and have done nothing to enhance their reputation.

Here the fan blades have been highlighted with graphite using a 2B pencil.

No amount of clamping and hot water would coerce the left wing into its characteristic droop.

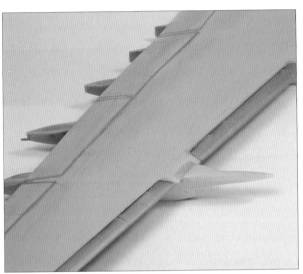

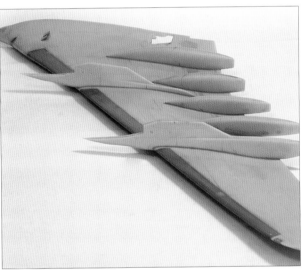

Heller decided to make the forward wing slats separate and moulded silver while the rest of the wing is grey. They're not positionable and require much trimming and filling to get a good fit. Note the amount of putty required around the engine pylon to get a flush fit.

The pylons weren't a great fit either and this time I've simply used repeated applications of any grey acrylic as a filler. Excess can be removed with methylated spirit without harm to the plastic surface.

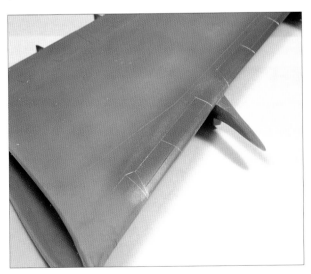

Slats have been painted SMS Silver Lacquer prior to masking for the main colour.

A short length of 1mm brass tube has been grafted in place for the fuel dump pipe.

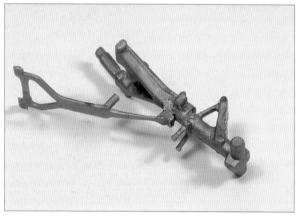

The much simplified nose gear before a little scratch building helped beef it up.

Wheels and tyres ready for fitting. Hubs sprayed Tamiya X-2 White and the centre hubs hand-painted Humbrol Silver.

Heller have elected to make the tyres out of a soft rubber type compound and these have been cut from their sprue leaving an ugly attachment point that's impossible to remove. Once fitted to the model, this isn't so obvious if in contact with the ground.

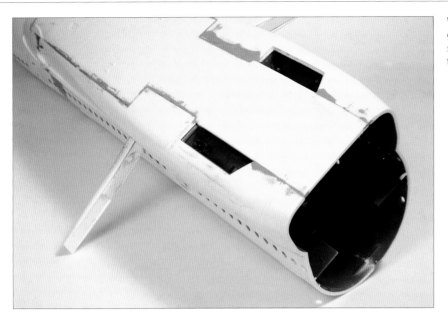

Wheel wells and interior painted dark grey. The fuselage is made up of five sections and these all need much filling, adding to the work load.

Tamiya putty basic type was used throughout for all filling. It's easy to work with, dries quickly and sands easily.

Only the cockpit windscreen is provided, decals cover the passenger windows. These were also filled in with Testors Clear to add support to the decals.

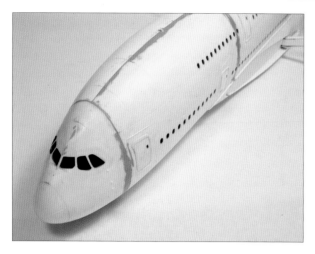

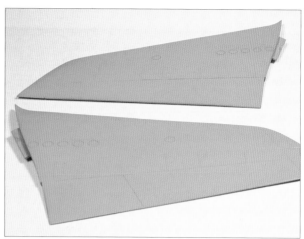

The cockpit interior is hardly visible even with these relatively large windows.

Tail surfaces painted Tamiya XF-14 J.A.

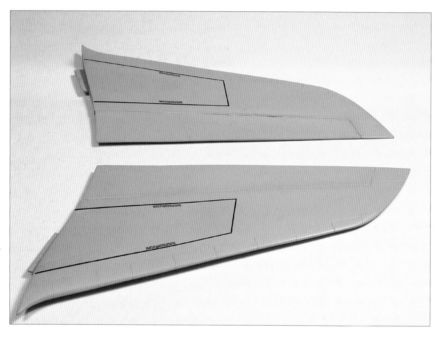

The control surfaces are mould solid with the lower half and leave quite a gap. This one was missed and required another fill, sand and repaint.

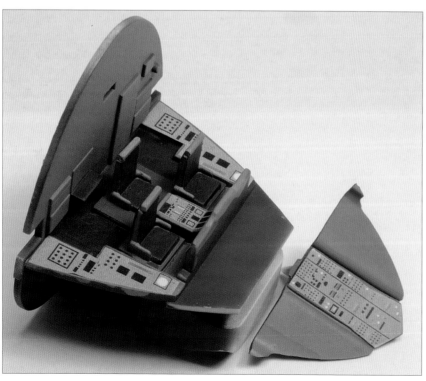

A basic cockpit with decals is provided but not much can be seen when closed up. I've added headrests from thick card.

Repeated filling and sanding was needed here as these fuselage parts were warped.

First layer of Tamiya White Primer has been polished ready for gloss coats.

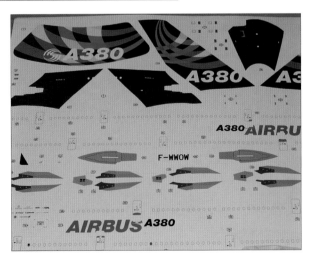

The windscreen isn't moulded well – even with the nodes there are still some deep sink marks and soft edges – and wasn't used. Instead, Testors Clear part adhesive filled in the frames.

A large comprehensive decal sheet provides all that's needed and is well laid out. Heller also provide a large solid stand for a table display model if required and that's where decal #1 comes in. The window frames are printed in various lengths and some of these had to be separated into twos and threes as the spacing wasn't quite right.

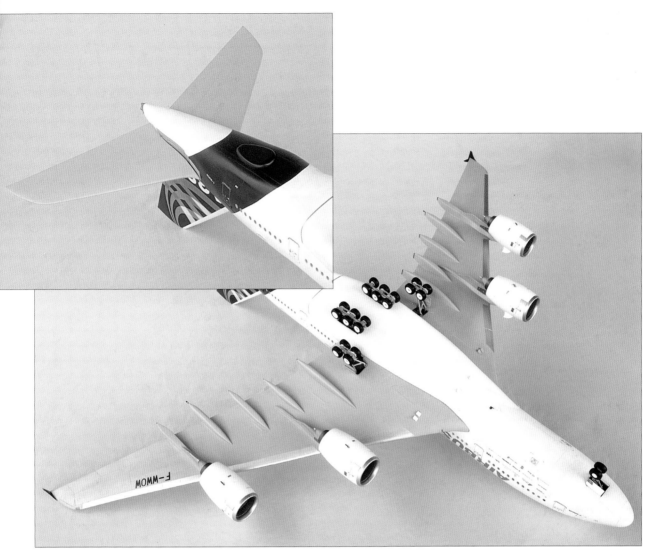